PROVOCACIONES
Letters from the Prettiest Girl in Arvin

by
Rafaela G. Castro

Louise,
You've been an
inspiration to me for our
forty years!

Con Cariño
Rafaela

ISBN: 1-891823-10-8

Library of Congress Control Number: 2006931884

Cover Illustration
Sylvia Savala

Graphic Design and Typography
Orange Frog Design • www.o-frog.com

Chusma House Publications
P.O. Box 467 • San José, CA 95103
phone: (408) 947-0958
email: chusmahouse@earthlink.net
www.chusmahouse.com

First Printing
Patsons Media Group
Sunnyvale, California

IN MEMORY OF

Dolores Gonzales Castro
1922 - 1997

and
Martín Duran Castro
1921 - 1993

Rafaela G. Castro

ACKNOWLEDGEMENT

I must express genuine gratitude to two organizations from the University of California, Davis campus. Both the Chicana Latina Research Center and the Librarian's Association of the University of California (LAUC), awarded me summer grants that permitted me to receive release time to work on this writing. I am super grateful to my sisters, Elva and Linda, who have supported me through the years by listening, providing stories, and reading my drafts. Two special friends, Elsa and Clint, listened patiently to many stories and I am indebted to them for their friendship and thoughtfulness. My faithful family, John, Solange, and Laura, have always been by my side, sustaining me with love, courage, and inspiration.

TABLE OF CONTENTS

PROVOCACIONES
Letters from the Prettiest Girl in Arvin

by
Rafaela G. Castro

SENTIMENTAL JOURNEY

I have a photograph of a formal portrait of our family taken to commemorate the twenty-fifth wedding anniversary of my mother and father. Sitting for a family portrait is an honorable sign of respectability, prosperity and stability; it reflects security in a home with a father, a mother and three beautiful daughters. It is still a handsome photograph, in a color tone called sepia that gives it a classic antique appearance. It has always hung on a prominent wall in all of the homes where I've lived. For close to forty years I have, almost daily, looked at and scrutinized this photo, putting my nose up close to study the facial expressions of my parents and sisters. As the years increase and pile up, the more I intimately examine the clothes, the hairdos, the postures, wonder about the smiles, and strive to decipher the thoughts in each person's head. The photograph crystallizes a fleeting period, a short but proud and glorious time in the history of my family. All the dreams, aspirations, and goals of all of us are frozen at this very moment in this photograph.

Lola and Martín didn't want a big celebration, no

parties, no dinners, nothing that would draw attention to us, to them. Instead, on that anniversary Saturday in February of 1963, the five of us, dressed in our best, went to a very early Mass at St. Patrick's church, and to breakfast at the International House of Pancakes. Then we went home and posed before a professional photographer. The photographer came to our house and took several sittings, making us all nervous, yet I think we were happy. It was a peaceful time, a tranquil moment, and a lull before the occurrence of major dramatic changes in the lives of each one of us.

In the photo Lola and Martín are seated, his left arm around her shoulders is resting on the back of her chair and we, the three daughters are dutifully standing behind them. My father looks very handsome in a dark suit, with his thin moustache perfectly trimmed, his head slightly leaning towards the right, wearing his eye glasses he liked to wear when he dressed up, yet didn't quite need on a daily basis. I always thought he was an especially good-looking man, in his prime here at forty-two years of age. Although I imagine he was tense, he has a relaxed assured look with a steady gaze in his eyes and a small confident smile on his lips. I used to love to see him smile, with a humorous flash in his eyes, visible for only a second as they would start to close when he laughed. It was a comforting look, safe, and it gave me a secure feeling, glad that he wasn't mad. We never knew when he'd be angry.

My mother is wearing an attractive but conservative chocolate brown suit with a white frilly blouse. Her suit has that Jackie Kennedy look to it, a straight skirt with a short waist length jacket. The frilly lace around the high collar of the blouse softens the formality of the suit. Her dark hair, in a short bouffant, is very stylish and of the times, but the dark rimmed glasses she is wearing appear too large, the frames too thick. Surprisingly she isn't wearing jewelry, no earrings, only a gold flower broach on the lapel of her jacket that must have been a Mother's Day gift. She would always admonish us for not wearing earrings, telling us not to look like boys, yet here she is not following her own advice. Lola was not a pretty woman, but she always looked attractive and smart. She possessed an innate elegance that carried her through any situation. Even when she worked in the hot agricultural fields, she would wear make- up, cologne, and stylishly arrange her hair. She loved colognes, fashionable clothes, and pretty shoes. Here, she is dressed in her best, but her fragile smile is awkward, nervous, almost fearful.

It was because of the photographer. He made them, made all of us feel tense and uncomfortable. He was *un americano*, a white man, an intruder in our home. Our balance of order was disrupted whenever a white person came into our house. English would have to be spoken by Lola and Martín, and a certain decorum was imposed on us all. Our home life was always somewhat rigid, but it was a sheltered and protective environment, especially during our teenage years, after we'd left Arvin and moved to northern California. Our family relations then were limited to our five-member family unless, we drove to Bakersfield to visit grandparents, uncles, aunts, and cousins. We always enjoyed the periods when our cousins came north to stay with us in the summers, sometimes for weeks at a time. There was an unspoken loneliness about our lives, and they alleviated it. My sisters and I had friends, but my mother and father had few. Our girlfriends were our school friends or our telephone friends, and only a small number were able to pierce into our family bastion and be accepted by Lola. Boyfriends had a terrible time breaking into the impenetrable silent fortress created by Martín. Why did we bring this *extranjero* into this sanctuary to take an imprint of our lives? It seems so inappropriate of us, almost irresponsible, and the look on Lola's face says it all. It is not the face of her daily life, the face I loved, the face I have inscribed in my memory today.

But on that day she was in our hands. The idea of a visiting photographer was probably that of my eldest sister, Chata. We always thought she aspired to be in a higher social class than we could ever attain. Not necessarily more acculturated and less Mexican but more worldly and sophisticated. Having a professional photographer come into our home was a very high-class, *jaitón*, kind of thing to do, besides probably being rather expensive. I wonder if Lola and Martín had anything to say about it, for we were the ones who orchestrated the day, and yet today I am glad of it. We have this still life, this captured presence of a family that felt much love and interdependence. It is an instant in time that we can place our happiness on, a moment that gave our family the appearance of being joyful. But there were anxieties raging inside the hearts of all of us. This home would be very different one year from the date of this prestigious *retrato*.

Lola and Martín left for Reno that Saturday afternoon for a weekend alone. They had never done this before, never in all the twenty-five years of their marriage. They had never gone away for a weekend to stay in a motel, to eat in restaurants, and be alone with each other. Such a trip, although not a great extravagance, was still an indulgence and commemorated this important event. They rarely had opportunities for amusement and didn't know how to enjoy themselves, except for dancing. Dancing was their main entertainment. They loved to dance and did it well together. There was one local Mexican club they frequented for drinks and dancing, and they attended holiday dances for New Years in Vallejo or Oakland. Or they invited their few friends to come over for food, drinks and always dancing. The four-hour drive to Reno, for the weekend, was a premium reward, especially for Lola, who had persisted in the marriage in spite of the many humiliating experiences she had experienced in it.

We, the daughters, knew little of the tumultuous love story behind the marriage of our parents. Our naiveté would soon be shattered, but on this particular day everyone was thrilled. For a teenager, it was exciting to celebrate one's parents' twenty-fifth wedding anniversary. They were in love, this I know, that they always loved each other. On this day we felt a sense of elegance, of pride in our *familia*, and we were fortunate to have the money to send them to Reno. Financially, it was a prosperous time for our family. All five of us were employed full time and each of us handed over half of our paycheck to Lola, except for Martín; he handed over all of his biweekly check.

We were left alone that weekend, alone without a chaperone. This had never happened before either, even though the eldest of us was twenty-three years of age. Once or twice Lola and Martín had gone away to Bakersfield or Texas for a family emergency, such as an illness or a funeral, and they had asked the mother-in-law of the Mexican neighbor across the street to look in on us. She may have even spent the night, sleeping in Lola's bed, even though we were in high school and my oldest sister was already working. The liberty they entrusted us with on this weekend showed they were beginning to accept us as adults or that they finally believed us trustworthy, or that they feared the outside world less. Being left alone was our reward.

Actually, we were more than grown-up. In some ways we were overly cautious little old ladies. We behaved like *señoritas viejas*, as some would say, afraid of the world and always expecting the worse. Reserved, shy, gravely responsible, proper in our manners, excessively organized, and disinclined to take risks, we were Lola's creations. Still, it felt good to be left alone in the house. We had moved into our new home five years previously and we loved its ordered immaculateness. I vaguely remember having a date that evening, something not totally normal. As the youngest of the three daughters, I somehow gained youthful freedoms at an earlier age and dated in a typical American way. On this occasion, I was going to dinner with the older brother of one of my best friends. He was from a good Catholic Portuguese family, a handsome but shy and uninteresting young man; however, it was a date.

My sister, the eldest, was soon to be married and probably spent the evening with her fiancé. They had become engaged the previous Christmas and were in the midst of planning an elaborate wedding in the tradition of their peers and the local community. But unlike local tradition, I, her sister, was to be the Maid of Honor. She and her fiancé were serious in their intended vows, were careful planners and were meticulously arranging the first most important day of their future life together. In the family portrait she is beautiful, sophisticated, confident in the safe future guaranteed her; a husband and babies are in the picture also, in her heart. Looking petite and pretty, she is situated at the exact center of the family setting. Wearing a tailored maroon colored dress, she is standing behind and directly between the seated Lola and Martín. Because the backdrop of the light colored drapes creates a strong contrast with the dark-haired heads of us, the standing daughters, the viewer's eye automatically lands in the middle, directly on her. She is the center of the photograph, and any observer will notice that here she appears to be in control, at least at this very moment. She often played this role in the family. Lola learned to look to her for guidance and advice. She was the eldest and wisest of her daughters and the one most educated in the ways of the public culture.

To her right stands my other sister Linda, the middle daughter. She looks rather worldly and wise with her beautifully made up face. Her arched penciled eyebrows convey self-acceptance and a certain flamboyance. Soon to be twenty-two, and although she hasn't informed us at this moment, soon to be married. Who knows what is going through her heart? Wearing a black brocade dress, her shoulder length hair is perfectly coiffured, her eyes lavishly made up, her spirited personality apparent. Her smile, in a near smirk, hints of things she knows. She has a burning secret that will soon burst upon us. In a few months she must tell Lola and Martín, and what a shock it will be to them.

I remember that quick trip to Reno in the snow when she married her Mexican lover. Very soon they had a lovely dark-eyed doll even before the wedding day of our older sister. It was a huge disappointment for Lola and Martín, even though they did receive a granddaughter that melted their anger and swelled their hearts with love. This lovely baby girl catapulted the dynamics of a serene family of five into indulging, mushy, baby-talking grown-ups.

I, the youngest, am on the right side of the portrait, left of my eldest sister, appearing very 1960s with a full bouffant hairstyle and a slightly open, teeth displayed, smile. Because of my hair-do, I appear to be the tallest of the three of us. My knit suit is dark brown, very appropriate for church, but for a family portrait? It isn't apparent here, but I am just following along with the program, doing as I'm told, but with my head in other places. Still thinking like a teenager, I have no marriage plans, no baby plans, and no boyfriend; actually I have no future. My sisters had always been my role models, but here they are fashioning a path that I wasn't ready to follow. In my youthful and impetuous outspokenness, I often criticized their life choices. I am wearing a thin multi-strand gold necklace that stands out in the photo because I'm the only one wearing jewelry. Even an indifferent observer will notice a striking feature of this family portrait, how proper and dignified we all appear, solemn even, especially for such a young family. I doubt this was meant to be such a serious moment.

We celebrated their anniversary that Saturday, feeling

blessed and contented with our lives and with the world. My sisters already knew, but it was many months or even years before I somehow learned that in the year 1939, and not in 1938 as we'd been told, Lola and Martín had a civil marriage in February and then a religious ceremony in May at St. Patrick's Church in Canutillo, Texas. Their first daughter was born the very next month, in June. I am not even sure that I understood the significance of this information. There were other secrets too, secrets that were important and necessary for the family because they provided the driving energy that kept it together. Without such secrets, Lola probably would not have worked so hard to keep the marriage intact. These days I derive subtle pleasure from studying this photograph, knowing that secret thoughts are well concealed behind those unsure smiles and earnest eyes. It isn't maliciousness on my part, but just a special enjoyment I experience in realizing that the people in the photo are not the people I thought I knew when I was a young girl. They are somewhat flawed but yet more interesting, more complex and saturated with contradictions that urge me to probe deeper into their past lives.

Lola and Martín loved each other passionately and it was physical passion that forced them into marriage as teenagers. For most of their lives they understood each other and shared a mutual respect although at times it was clear an imbalance existed in their relationship. Martín was recklessly good looking with charm and wit. Lola looked lovely when stylishly dressed up, with her face made-up, but she was a plain woman. As a little girl, she wore rimless glasses from the age of ten, and she did not stand out among the other girls, yet there was an intrinsic refinement and grace about her. What was it that attracted them to each other? Martín was very handsome from the time he was a young teenager until his death at age 72. Although not a tall man he was robust and with his dark hair, dark skin and strong white teeth, he exuded boldness, arrogance and confidence. But, Lola was much smarter; she was sharp, shrewd, quick, money-wise, a take-charge-of-a-situation type person. Wherever they lived, she could make a home; have clean clothes and a full meal on the table in a matter of hours. Martín adored her, he needed her, and she loved him. Often, we'd find them hugging in the kitchen with Martín's hand briefly resting on her backside as he reached for her. They must have made passionate love; but Martín also looked at other women, and they looked at him.

Sometime in the year following this celebration, as I reached the ripe age of twenty, I experienced an existential crisis and I didn't quite know what to do with myself. My world was rapidly transforming and slipping out of the control I thought I had over it. I was no longer a teenager and felt I was being impolitely nudged into growing up and becoming responsible. In 1964, "growing up" for girls meant only one thing: marriage. My high school friends were either married or planning weddings, and a few were already having babies! Besides marriage, there were not many options available for a female high school graduate. I wanted something unknown, something indefinable, something exciting and challenging. What I wanted was adventure. I needed to experience a grand provocation. I liked the Spanish sound of it; *una gran provocación*. Something that would challenge me to become a different person, a new being! Of course I didn't know what it could be, but I knew I needed to be lifted, physically removed from my young lackadaisical life. Unfortunately, I wasn't talented, couldn't write, couldn't sing, dance, act, and could only play the French horn so the entertainment world did not call to me. I feared that if I didn't find a passion soon, I might suddenly perceive marriage as an attractive option and misinterpret it as my *gran provocación*. To me, marriage was that last door, way, way down at the end of a long corridor, a corridor that ended with only one Big Door. The door had a capital M on it, but the corridor was fully lined with many, many beautifully multi-colored doors on both sides of it. I wanted to open and explore all of the enticing side doors before I reached that last formidable one. My grandmother had a *dicho* she often shared with us when discussing marriage. *El matrimonio es la cruz de la mujer*, she'd say, scaring me to death and affirming my goal to search elsewhere for grand provocations.

My two sisters married and moved out of our home in the same year, shortly after our family portrait was taken, leaving me alone with my mother and father. I didn't envy the choices they had made, but it didn't feel right that I should be left alone so abruptly. My position in the family hierarchy shifted, and it was very disconcerting. I had been at the bottom, not totally ignored but left pretty much to my own schemes, and now I was the center of my parents' attention. They were saddened and comfortless, and our home life was morbidly different. There was a sad quietness in the house, more like a somber silence. With two of their daughters gone, my parents felt lonely, with a loss of direction in their lives, and they were dragging me along their path of melancholy.

The dental lab job I had once thought interesting now bored me terribly. I started investigating new options for myself and even considered joining the military because I wanted to travel, to see other countries, to encounter great mysteries and escapades. Attending college never entered my mind because I thought only rich or very smart kids went to college, and I was neither. Somehow, I don't know how, I stumbled onto the idea of joining the Peace Corps. Like many of my generation, I was an avid John F. Kennedy devotee. One hot night during the summer of 1960 stands out sharply in my mind as I was sitting on our living room floor playing solitaire and watching the Democratic convention on television as JFK was nominated. Like my parents I was rooting for Adlai Stevenson because he was a well-known Democrat supported by most Mexican Americans, yet we quickly came to love Kennedy when we learned of his Catholic background. My grandmother adored him because he gave back to Mexico the Texas stretch of land known as *El Chamizal*. In fact she was positive that this action alone was the reason for his assassination in Texas. That soulless day in November when he died, my boss, in a state of shock, closed the dental lab and sent me home. I went to the nearest Catholic Church and along with hundreds of other people, prayed and cried for several hours. Then I went home and sat in front of the television, sadly eating the sack lunch my mother always prepared for me and cried for the rest of the afternoon. Although I thought it far from my social and educational reach, JFK's Peace Corps became my goal, my challenge and soon my adventure. Gradually my future life started to take form and became intelligible to me. In my naïve mind, my plan was to leave my small home town for two years, travel, mature, perform extraordinarily good deeds for poor people in other countries, return home and marry my high school boyfriend, have babies, and then be like everyone else in my town. In other words, fulfill my gender and social destiny.

While I completed the 12-page application for the Peace Corps, took the many exams that tested my intelligence, exams that tested my Spanish language proficiency, medical and physical exams at the Mare Island Naval Base that checked my health and stamina, I considered how I was going to present this idea to Lola and Martín. They would never ever understand, approve, or bestow their blessing upon my decision. My sisters had lived at home until they married. All of my cousins, male and female, lived at home until they married. To leave one's parents' home for any reason other than marriage was unheard of in our family.

For a young woman of any age to leave home was almost a blasphemous act in any Catholic Mexican family. I realized I had to plot out a strategy. The previous summer, at the age of nineteen, I had managed to get approval for a two-week vacation in Hawaii, another unheard of event. Even my sisters had to respect my tactics in getting Martín to give me his blessing for that trip. By living very frugally, since I gave half of my meager earnings to my mother, I managed to save enough money to join three of my high school girlfriends on a very glamorous trip to Hawaii. I paid for everything in advance, the airline tickets, the tour to three islands, the hotels; and three weeks before the date of the trip, I presented the whole plan to Martín. He was so impressed with my monetary planning, and because I had non-refundable airline tickets, he couldn't help but give me his consent. Secretly, I think he was proud of me since I was known among my sisters as the tightwad of the family. If I had twenty cents in my pocket, I always managed to save at least ten cents. It was this grand Hawaii vacation that intensified my enthusiasm about seeking other wonderful provocations.

How could I ask for permission to travel to South America for two years? I didn't expect consent so I didn't intend to ask for permission. Instead when I approached Lola and Martín, I described the work of the Peace Corps, I spoke of the social policies of the Catholic John Kennedy, and reminded them that I had a special talent. Since I could speak Spanish, I explained, I could really help poor people in South America, although I don't remember if we actually valued our bilingualness at that time. I calmly and quietly slipped in the information that I had already mailed an application to the Peace Corps. I didn't know of course if I'd be accepted, and even if I was, I couldn't know if I'd even pass the strenuous three month training program that I'd read so much about. It was very possible that I wouldn't pass it. My father said nothing, but my mother had no doubts. "*¡Usted tiene la sangre muy débil!* Oh, you'll never pass the training, you'll get sick because you're not strong enough," were her words.

My sisters were very supportive. Perhaps they had already learned that another kind of life existed out there somewhere, a life that didn't require marriage. The rest of my extended family was dumbfounded, and one of my cousins skeptically asked me, "Aren't you afraid to leave your mother?" She didn't mean afraid for my mother; she meant afraid to be without my mother, to live away from her. I felt a bit contrite, but in my heart I felt no uncertainty about my decision. It was the right time. My grandmother came to stay with us a few days before I left for the training program in New Mexico, to console my mother, to pray for me and give me her *bendición*, and also to point out to me the momentous action I was taking. I have a small photo, taken on the day I left for Albuquerque, of her and I standing together in front of our house. My short body towers over her tiny frame, and I'm holding a black raincoat over my left arm with my right arm around her small shoulders. We are not smiling, and she is staring seriously into the camera.

I felt doomed. On that same day, right before we were to leave for the airport, the mail man delivered a letter from my *Tía Ruma*, Lola's sister, telling me that she was praying I'd change my mind and decide not to go. "*Mija, no se vaya, no deje a su mamá,*" was the phrase that I guiltily carried in my heart as we all sadly, and in silence, drove across the Bay Bridge to the San Francisco airport.

All three daughters were now metaphorically absent from the family portrait.

essay 2

ARVIN

Sometimes I'm awakened at dawn and think I'm hearing music from a Mexican radio station and sensing the movements of my mother in the kitchen. It is still dark, but the kitchen light is reflected on our bedroom door and across the doorway. On the radio, *una ranchera* is rousingly sung by a *conjunto mexicano*. I can faintly smell the aromas of coffee brewing and flour *tortillas* cooking on the *comal*. Whiffs of fried eggs, and of potatoes frying with onion and green *chile* float throughout the house and into our room. In my drowsy state I think, 'she's making my dad's lunch', and I blissfully roll over. Hallucinatory experiences like these happen often to me and continually draw me back into my childhood. So many times when returning home from school, I'd find my mother ironing, her neat stacks of pressed linens, starched shirts, and other clothes placed around the living room while she listened and sang along to the music of *Los Tres Diamantes*, *Lola Beltran*, or *Pedro Infante*. These illusive but comforting sensations originate in some deep psychic pocket of mine, and form a foundation from which I can always gather sustenance and potency.

Lola was a whirlwind that never stood still, slowed down, or ever vanished, existing simultaneously in every room of our small house. She worked incessantly and was constantly moving, in the kitchen, in the house, in the fields, in packing sheds, in factories, and eventually in her married daughters' homes. Every household chore, cleaning, cooking, from laundry to shopping was approached with a fixed determination that made it the most important task in the world. This was a fact to her. She could never have dirty dishes in the sink, unwashed laundry in the hamper, unironed clothes in her closet, or dust on the coffee table. Eventually she learned to enjoy and appreciate other daily pleasures, but for many years her primary ones consisted of a full day of hard labor, a very clean home and her motherly and wifely obligations fulfilled. And the same was expected of her daughters, but some of us disappointed her terribly.

Although born in the twentieth century, Martín was from another time, another world order and never quite made the transition into the world of the New Southwest. He should have been one of *Pancho Villa's Dorados*, or one of his lieutenants, or possibly *un hacendado*. He believed that as the eldest son, and as a man, he possessed absolute rights, privileges, and responsibilities. This meant that he reigned over his mother, his wife, children, and siblings, not so much as a king, but more like a *mayordomo*, a position he'd held many times as a farm worker. For most of our lives, we felt abused by his feudalistic viewpoint and behavior and it is only today that I can comprehend what he bequeathed to my upbringing and to my life.

When he walked into our house, we felt a formidable shake just as if an earthquake had hit us. As the house shook, we would start to tremble anticipating a command or an outburst. I was forever afraid of him. Everyone was afraid of him. When he spoke, the windows rattled, his voice a powerful low rumble that consistently sounded as if he were angrily shouting orders. He was, to my sisters and me; he liked ordering us around to show his friends and relatives what good, loyal and obedient daughters we were. Of course, as a young girl, I didn't know what a softy he would eventually become.

From his old world belief system, he insisted on a strict and structured home. Our family had dinner together every single night the minute he entered the door, which meant my mother had to have a ready dinner on the table. We could rarely leave the house in the evening. We were always in his presence, and if we weren't, there had to be a very good reason for it. Evening visits to our friends' homes were rare. Sexual jokes could not be told in his presence, nor bodily functions ridiculed. He was almost puritanical in his sexual values and outlooks and wouldn't allow my mother to be seen in shorts while in public, nor his daughters to wear suggestive clothing. And even though ours was a household of women, we always ran around the house carefully clothed. Yet, he was unfaithful to Lola.

As teenagers our lives were neatly partitioned between home and school. Any extracurricular activities we might have were associated with school, and sometimes with The Church. During Lent we attended Mass together every morning, and although this was Lola's edict, Martín went along too. What I gained from this environment was security, confidence, and a strong sense of family pride. We were shy and reserved girls, yet we shared a respectfulness and a closeness among ourselves that is rare and difficult to explain. I had no problem comparing my family home life with that of any of my friends.

Lola, baptized Dolores, was fair and light-skinned, and often called *la Güera*. My *Tío* Jim, who gave everyone a nickname, frequently called her *la Okie*, a name that some might find disparaging. Martín, although a young man in his thirties, became stocky and picked up the nickname of *el*

Gordo, which quickly became a title that connoted awe and fear to all that met him. Lola and Martín taught us by example; they rarely preached or lectured us. From my father, I learned to be a loyal and hard working employee, to respect older people, to value education, and to love my family, including all of my second and third cousins. From my mother, I learned to be strong, resourceful, frugal, to have faith, to be continuously busy and well organized, keep a clean home, and to be suspicious of all men.

As a three or four year old, I contracted an unknown skin disease on my scalp. My mother described it to me by just stating that, *tenía granos en la cabeza,* maybe it was ringworm or lice, which were unavoidable among the poor Okies and Mexicans in those days. Whatever the malady, it was necessary that my hair be cut and my head completely shaved. I was totally bald and for a few months became unique, asexual, or in modern terms non-gendered. Without a full head of hair, my sexual identity could not be determined. The *braceros* that lived with us as boarders teased me saying I looked like a boy, and they would call me *muchachito*, or Pablito, a name that I instantaneously abhorred. I would argue furiously that I was not a boy although even at that very young age I instinctively knew boys had more fun than girls. For at least the next twenty years, whenever I wore my hair very short, the name Pablito would materialize in conversations with my sisters, mother, grandmother, and other relatives. It may have been during this period that whenever we visited our relatives in Bakersfield, my *Tío* Jim, perhaps in an attempt to make me feel better, would say to me, *"Ay viene la muchacha más bonita de Arvin."* Or he'd ask me, *"¿Quién es la muchacha más bonita de Arvin?"* I don't remember how I answered him. I knew he was kidding me; besides, everybody knew there couldn't be many pretty girls in a town like Arvin.

Situated in the southeastern corner of the San Joaquin

Valley, with its population of approximately 4,000 in-town residents, Arvin was not an impressive municipality in the late 1940s. Actually it was more of an agricultural village and because of high unemployment and few economic opportunities, my family eventually moved away in 1953. Through one of his many cousins, my father obtained permanent employment and a good union job in a smelting and refining factory in the Bay Area of northern California. We relocated to a strange world of hills and rain, very different from the one we had left behind; our housing was very different, the climate, the milieu, the people, and the language. Gradually we also became transformed. But Arvin, the little colony, remained in our hearts and in our psyches forever. It was the site of our early history, and we could never fully erase it from our memory. Through the years as we looked back on our past and childhood, Arvin became a symbol of our social innocence, unawareness and scant sophistication. As adults, each in our own individual melancholic state, we must have eventually acknowledged that Arvin was a metaphor for our eternal *mexicanidad*, our Mexicanness.

Arvin earned a somewhat poignant status in California history during the 1930s and 1940s although it was for events that entirely overlooked or more truthfully, disregarded its Mexican population. John Steinbeck's *The Grapes of Wrath*, his novel depicting the insufferable California journey of an Oklahoma family, was published to great acclaim in 1939. The government farm labor camp called Wheatpatch in the novel, where the Joad family settles for a short time, was located just a few miles outside of Arvin. Originally called Arvin Federal Migratory Camp, today it is named Sunset Camp and has been in continuous operation, during harvest season, since 1936. The Hollywood version of the novel was filmed at the same labor camp. Steinbeck's portrayal of the Okie Dust Bowl migrants, their poverty, language and objectionable behavior caused a nation-wide uproar, and it was especially noisy up and down the San Joaquin Valley. So loud was the clamor that the book was banned and even publicly burned in several cities. It wasn't out of sympathy for the Okies that the local communities, such as the Associated Farmers of Kern County, objected to *The Grapes of Wrath*, but rather it was because of the attention the book brought to the abysmal living conditions and the agricultural industry's wretched treatment of agricultural workers. The novelistic portrayal of the violence associated with farm workers organizing and striking for better wages was not well received by the large local farm corporations either. Of course there were also major objections to Steinbeck's socialist inclinations, and there was a common belief that through his writings he was advocating for communist resolutions.

Arriving in the region in late 1940, I'm almost certain Lola and Martín were unaware of the social and literary debates surrounding *The Grapes of Wrath*, and I wonder how much real contact they had with Okies. We know most of the people they worked with, in the fields and in the packing sheds, were Mexican. They first lived in the labor camp of the Di Giorgio Fruit Corporation where the company policy was to segregate the tenants. That is, the Okies lived in one section, the Mexicans in another, the Filipinos in another, and the Japanese workers in a totally separate camp. This same policy applied to the fields and packing shed jobs as well, where the workers were segregated by work assignments. Usually the Mexicans and Filipinos worked in the scorching fields, while the white men drove the tractors and trucks or worked indoors in the sheds. After they left the Di Giorgio farm, both Lola and Martín eventually became crew leaders, and each had a group of workers they were responsible for. Martin had men and Lola had women. I imagine it was because they were bilingual and could communicate with both the growers and the workers that they were thrust into what, at that time, were considered respectable and responsible payroll positions.

There was another socioeconomic controversy that propelled Arvin into the political limelight of California during the 1940s. It involved the research and publication of a government study that examined the impact of corporate industrial farming on rural communities of the San Joaquin Valley. The principal investigator, Walter Goldschmidt, was employed by the Bureau of Agricultural Economics of the U.S. Department of Agriculture. Published in 1946, the primary inquiry of the report was to look at the effects of corporate agriculture on the character of life in rural America. But the underlying public policy issue being examined was very basic; cheap public water for agribusiness. The Central Valley Project of California, subsidized by federal funds, was being developed, and at stake was the question of who was eligible to receive irrigation water from this program. The Reclamation Act of 1902 provided that irrigation water developed through federal subsidies would be allocated to family size farms of no more than 160 acres, and the huge looming question was whether this law should apply to the Central Valley Project.

For his comparative study of rural communities, Goldschmidt selected two small agricultural towns; one was Dinuba in Tulare County and the other was our little windswept desert town of Arvin in Kern County. These two communities were apparently very similar according to historical, social, and economic measurements, except that the sizes of the farms surrounding each town were different. Dinuba had a larger number of small independent family owned farms, while mostly large industrial farming corporations such as the Di Giorgio Fruit Corporation surrounded Arvin. After analyzing the data collected,

Goldschmidt concluded that small-scale farms fostered a higher quality of life in agricultural rural communities. His study showed that the effects of corporate farming in the Arvin area ensured that a higher number of people would be dependent upon seasonal wage labor and that the population would be more transitory and less stable. Consequently, the standard of living would be substantially lower. In addition, social institutions such as schools, parks, churches, and community centers were poorer, as well as the physical facilities of the town, like paved streets, sidewalks, sewage disposal, and so forth. In contrast, small farm communities provided more opportunity for private business enterprises, for increased retail trade in town, and for freer social integration of the various social groups. In general, a small farm community had more institutions for democratic decision-making and provided civic opportunities for participation by all its citizens.

There was much local opposition to Goldschmidt's research from the very beginning, and the study's conclusions caused an enormous disturbance that was not welcomed by agribusiness, nor by the Kern County Chamber of Commerce. The farmlands that were to benefit from the Central Valley Project were those owned by the giant agricultural corporations in the region, and the findings that these same corporations were actually a detriment to the economic and social life of their local communities brought them attention they could do without. Goldschmidt was venomously attacked, and a concerted effort was launched to suppress his research and final report. In fact enough sufficient political pressure was applied so that the U.S. Department of Agriculture backed off from publishing it. It was tabled for two years before it was salvaged and published by the Senate Small Business Committee, and not by the Department of Agriculture. The Arvin-Dinuba Study, as it has come to be known in California agricultural economics, has a long history and it is still cited in national discussions of farm consolidation and water rights. It need not to be stated, especially to those who know California, that the Central Valley Project has been delivering water for over fifty years to large agriculture corporations that own land on the very green western side of the San Joaquin Valley, an area devoid of small farms and rural communities.

From the data collected and analyzed in the Arvin-Dinuba study we're presented with a vivid, albeit desolate picture of the Arvin community of 1940. From my early childhood memories, I can still envision crowds of Mexican children in school and in town, but in reality, we made up a very small percentage of the total population, a measly 6%. In fact our numbers were considered so insignificant that Goldschmidt himself casually dismissed us with the statement, "the effect of alien cultures on the character of the two communities is negligible." (*As you Sow*, 1978, p.291) His rendition of alien cultures did not just refer to us Mexican people, but also to the Native American, Chinese, Japanese and Filipino populations that lived in the area. Arvin was settled in 1908 by four homesteading families that came from San Bernardino to establish a farming community. Grapes and cotton were introduced in the 1920s, but the area grew slowly, and it wasn't until the 1930s that a grand portion of Arvin was developed. Native Californians were a minority in 1944. 77% of the population had arrived after 1935 and 53% after 1940. Lola and Martín were a fraction of this 53% arriving in late 1940. These were the years of the Great Depression and the new arrivals were mostly poor people from the states of Oklahoma, Texas, Missouri and Kansas. Interestingly, the expeditious progression of agricultural production in the area mirrored the swift influx of the population with 74% of fruitful acres coming into production after 1936. In 1919 the Di Giorgio Fruit Company bought 19,000 acres north of

Rafaela G. Castro

Arvin, but it was from 1937 to 1943 that 17,000 acres were developed in the outer areas surrounding Arvin. In the fall of 1936, John Steinbeck wrote a series of incendiary articles about the Dust Bowl migrants for the *San Francisco News*. His first article states "at least 150,000 homeless migrants [are] wandering up and down the state." Two years later the preface to a pamphlet form of these same articles stated, "There are now more than 250,000 homeless migrants in the agricultural fields of California." From today's perspective it is blatantly apparent that the Great Depression was remarkably beneficial to the growth of California's agricultural industry.

I try to imagine how Arvin appeared to Lola and Martín in the 1940s when they first settled there. Were they eager to start a new life in "the great flat valley"? They were the newcomers, although unrecognized as part of the exodus Steinbeck wrote about. It is hard to believe they were so greatly outnumbered and that the town was made up of more white people than Mexican, more displaced workers than settled residents. Yet even as a child, I recall that everyone worked extremely hard to make a decent basic living. The lively child that I was, I have many happy memories of my early years there. I will never forget oppressive heat and the tarred burning streets; the new air-conditioned American, and the old dingy Mexican movie theatres; my small school shrouded in white fog throughout the winter; my First Communion dress and the medicinal smell of the Franciscan nuns who taught us catechism at St. Thomas Catholic Church; the Spring wildflowers in the foothills of the Tehachapi mountains; and all of my Mexican and Okie classmates. The commercial area of town was almost non-existent, and we drove to Bakersfield for most of our shopping. But sometimes we did shop at the Valley Mercantile store, have sodas at the soda fountain in the drugstore, and every Sunday and Thursday evening, our family went to see Mexican movies. My heart-throbs were *Pedro Infante, Cantinflas,* and *Pedro Armendariz.* For a period of time, we lived in very meager housing and were actually pretty poor, but through Lola's hard work and masterful planning, we eventually were able to acquire what we considered to be a spacious modern two-bedroom new house. In a land of impoverished nomads, our provincial lives flourished in a Spanish language enclave of Mexican workers.

Similar to the Joad family's migration to California on the great Mother Road, Lola and Martín journeyed to California in 1939 from Canutillo and La Union, two closely related rural communities located in different states, Texas and New Mexico. All their lives they proudly claimed loyalty to their birth states even though their towns were only five miles apart. They traveled in an old Model-T that had a rumble seat in the back, loaded down with personal belongings, three babies, a nine-year old boy, and four adults. There was Lola and Martín, their six-month-old baby, Lola's young brother, her sister and brother-in-law and their two babies. They attached a trailer to the car to carry all of their bedding, cooking utensils, and clothing. Martín and Johnny, the nine-year old, rode in the rumble seat. They didn't take Route 66, as the Joads had, but instead traveled on Highway 10, that wove through southern New Mexico and led to Highway 8 through southern Arizona and eventually into California. They camped along the way, the young men finding work wherever it was available. Lola and her sister were resourceful and industrious, having learned from their hard-working widowed mother how to manage a home, cook large meals, clean and take care of a family. At every encampment along the highway, they set up house, bringing out their pans and dishes, immediately cooking a pot of beans, and making stacks of *tortillas.* At one point they had to spend several weeks in Eloy, camped alongside the road because their car had broken down. The men, technically still teenagers, found work picking cotton, but only for a short while because there were a lot of other people camped along the road that were also looking for work. When the car was fixed, they were encouraged to travel to Calipatria, California where there was agricultural work picking peas, but that job didn't last long either. They also learned where they could receive government aid that included food staples, cigarettes, and even cash. Martín was mortified about accepting public assistance, but at certain times, he and Lola didn't have much choice. They stayed in a couple of other labor camps, but they did not remember the names of these camps well enough to recount them to their children. Eventually they made their way up to Anaheim where they found work and lived well for a short while.

It was now summer in 1940, Lola and her sister were pregnant again, and it was the men who made the decisions about what to do next. After a few weeks in California, Lola's brother-in-law, my *Tío* Jim, decided to return to Arizona, taking his wife and children and the car, leaving Lola and Martín in Anaheim. Everyone understood that Martín was too embarrassed to return to Canutillo because he had come to California to work and to live, and he would find a way. In August of that year, he put Lola and their baby daughter on the bus back to Texas, for a few months, he said, while he found work and housing. He then worked his way up north to visit his uncle, his father's brother who lived in the Di Giorgio farm labor camp near Arvin.

Martín was hired by the Di Giorgio Fruit Company and thus qualified for housing. The labor camp was a large compound of barrack structures located across a county road from the Di Giorgio train stop and packing shed, mid-way between Lamont and Arvin, two or three miles distant from each small rustic town. Hundreds of laborers, single men and whole families, lived in the labor camp, all judiciously segregated by their appropriate nationality. After the war started and the Emergency Farm Labor Program was instituted in 1942, there were Mexican *braceros* who worked for Di Giorgio and also lived in the labor camp. Living quarters for the families consisted of two rooms, a bedroom and a kitchen with no indoor plumbing. There were bathrooms, showers, and clothes washing facilities in a large rectangular structure situated between two long rows of barracks. The Di Giorgio compound must have looked pretty good to Martín, after months of camping and living in tents. He sent for Lola, and she arrived by Greyhound bus with their baby daughter and another younger sister, on November 30th 1940. Eventually all of Lola's and Martín's families migrated from Texas and New Mexico, and almost all of them initially moved into the Di Giorgio labor camp, some for a few months and some for several years.

In 1947, Arvin was again thrust into the public media when 1500 workers of the Di Giorgio Fruit Company walked out on strike. Some of the workers lived in the labor camp, but many lived in the surrounding rural areas and small towns like Lamont, Weedpatch, the Sunset labor camp, and Arvin. It was to be one of the longest farm labor strikes in California agribusiness history, lasting over two years. Although Martín's brother-in-law was involved in the strike, it had little or no significance in the lives of Lola and Martín, and they never spoke of it to us. It was a long drawn out nasty confrontation, violent at times, with one man shot and wounded in his home in Arvin as he held a union meeting. The state and federal governments became involved, conducting separate investigations, and the local community again received a great deal of attention from social reformers, communist fearing conservatives, Hollywood progressives, and university professors. The strike was featured in a documentary film made by the

Hollywood Film Council titled, "Poverty in the Valley of Plenty" that highlighted the main street of Arvin. The labor struggle reached a culmination when a congressional hearing was convened in Bakersfield in late 1949. A three member House of Representatives Education subcommittee conducted the hearings. One of its members was a freshman congressman who was later to become an important American historical figure, Richard Nixon. He left a lasting impression on several of the people present who have written about this bit of California history. The strikers were mostly white men and women, with only a few hundred Mexican workers supporting it. At the time, it was believed that Mexicans didn't want to join the Di Giorgio strike because during the famous cotton strike of 1933 many Okies had worked as scabs and undermined the Mexican strikers. The Di Giorgio strike has been well documented by various writers including the famous researcher Ernesto Galarza. As in other California farm labor strikes, the workers didn't have a chance against the large farm corporations that controlled local business interests and judicial forums in the San Joaquin Valley.

Even with the writings of John Steinbeck, the published reports of the U.S. Department of Agriculture written by university researchers and the publicity of congressional hearings, the plight of the farm worker continued to deteriorate in the 1940s, 1950s, and 1960s. It wasn't until the labor organizing efforts of Cesar Chavez and the United Farm Workers that the working conditions and employee rights of Mexican and Filipino farm workers received national attention and started to improve somewhat. By this time my mother and father were no longer working as farm laborers, but even if they had been, it is unlikely they would have supported the struggle of Cesar Chavez, for as Lola once told me, "*los rancheros nos trataban bien.*" She maintained a loyalty to the growers and believed they had been good to us.

All my life I have heard the name Di Giorgio and can still remember looking out the window of our car as we drove past the company's labor camp, the packing sheds and even his home on our drives from Arvin to Bakersfield. *"Allí está la casa de Di Giorgio,"* someone in the car would say and we'd all strain our necks to see it. The name conjured up images of a benevolent grandfatherly type man who helped many people, especially us Mexicans. I can remember as a five year-old going to a *jamaica* there and crying when a *cascarón* was broken over my head, and I have fuzzy blurry memories of my grandmother's home when she lived there. My great-grandmother lived in that labor camp, and both of my grandmothers, one for only a short time and the other for six or seven years. My grandfather died while he lived there and his brother, the *Tío* Bruno that lured Martín to California and to Di Giorgio, continued to work there for over twenty-five years. He advanced, moved out of farm work and became a plumber for Di Giorgio, earning the privilege of living in an actual house and not in a two-room compartment in the barracks. Eventually all of my relatives moved out and settled in modest housing in Bakersfield, Lamont or Arvin.

By the time I was born in late 1943, Lola and Martín no longer lived in Di Giorgio, in fact they'd already lived in a couple of different sites and were to continue to live an unstable life for several more years. We don't know, my sisters and I, what was happening to Martín during those years, but we do know that he had more than one extra-marital affair. He was in his early 20s, handsome, and Lola was either pregnant or overweight; there was much bickering and fighting between them in the first few years after my birth. He held various different jobs, working in a factory in Bakersfield, running a bar in Arvin, and always there was farm work. By late 1946 or maybe it was already

1947, their marriage became unbearable to both of them I assume, and Martín left the family. It pains me terribly even today to think of what my mother must have experienced. She was a young woman, twenty-four years old, with three young children, no secure source of income, and no man to support and love her. I ask myself: what was Martín thinking? I know what she thought, she had to take care of her daughters, but what did he think?

Lola was shrewd and strong and she followed her instincts. At the critical devastating point when Martín left her, she acted quickly. Because Martín no longer worked for the grower Kovacevich, she had to move out of employee housing, *en un rancho* where they were living in the outskirts of Arvin. She needed housing immediately and found it in Arvin, a funny looking structure that became known to us forever as *la casa de lamina*, because of its aluminum siding. It was a three and a-half room apartment, one end of a sort of duplex, located in an unpaved alley one and a half blocks north of Arvin's main street. My earliest childhood memories are of this house, and I remember it as large and roomy, but in reality, it was somewhat of a tiny shack. I don't recollect that we ever spoke to whomever lived at the other end of the small building. It had two tiny bedrooms, a kitchen, and a short hallway in front of the bathroom, which is where Josefina, a woman who had lived with us for sometime, slept on a cot. My mother and we three girls slept in one room, and she rented the other room to three Mexican workers, probably *braceros*. There was barely space in that room for the three World War II army cots. They paid Lola for room and board, and now I wonder if they weren't refugees from the Di Giorgio labor strike. In addition, there were at least two other men who came to our house just for their meals. I remember this, but I never asked my mother how this idea occurred to her nor how the arrangement developed. Lola and Josefina cooked for all the men, and Lola also worked in the fields. She was in charge of a crew of women that pruned vineyards and worked in the packing sheds of the local grower Guimara.

Every morning Lola and Josefina arose by 4:00 a.m. to make breakfast and lunches for the boarders. They'd start by making four or five dozen flour *tortillas*, and then they cooked eggs, potatoes, *chile*, and heated any leftover beans from the previous day's dinner. I've calculated that at 5:00 a.m. each man would eat three or four *tortillas* with breakfast. Lola would then make *burritos*, called *tacos* in those days, for their lunches, at least five or six per man, and for dinner, another four or five dozen *tortillas* had to be made. That is, each man could easily eat one dozen *tortillas* per day, and the rest of us in the family probably ate another couple of dozen. Each individual *tortilla* was hand rolled, with a makeshift rolling pin in the form of a piece of pipe, and individually cooked on a *comal*. It is staggering to imagine the number of *tortillas* made each day by Lola and Josefina during those years. At the end of the day, after working ten or more arduous hours in the fields or packing sheds, Lola rushed home, took a bath and started making dinner for the men and for us. During the day Josefina, with me as her little helper, would clean the house, cook a fresh pot of beans, and start the evening batch of *tortillas*. Lola was an excellent cook. She loved to experiment with different *chiles* and meats, combining various vegetables with *chiles*, and always providing huge quantities of food to the boarders. To guarantee that she'd never ran out of basic food staples; she'd purchase 100-pound sacks of flour, beans, onions, rice, and potatoes. The *braceros*, I can still recollect Cristóbal, Lupe and Don Sotero, loved her and her cooking. I doubt they had ever seen a woman, especially so young a woman, work as hard as she did. During this time her sisters didn't see her much and I guess neither did we.

I can barely resurrect shadowy memories of those years,

when I was three, four and five years old. Since my sisters were in school most of the day, I had Josefina all to myself, and we spent our days in conversation, moving about slowly as we did our chores. I assisted her as she washed the dishes, swept the floors, and cleaned the beans before placing them in a large pot for the evening meal. She always carried a monocle, in her pocket or around her neck that she placed over one eye as she sorted the beans, searching for the small clots of dirt. Because of the heat, and because the house was so small, I spent a lot of time outdoors playing or sitting on the front steps. One of our neighbors owned a beautiful colorful fierce *gallo* that strutted through the alley and ran freely around our small yard. He was a huge rooster, with a high red comb that made him almost as tall as I was, and he pursued me aggressively. He would jump on me, trying to spur me I suppose, and always managed to knock me down onto the dusty hot dirt. Terrified, I tried hard to stay away from him, but he didn't like me and sought me out whenever he could. Perhaps he thought I was a rival *gallo* since I was almost his same height. One day we were all getting dressed up for an occasion, possibly for Church; my mother bathed me and dressed me first, combed my hair, and made me feel especially smart. She scooted me outside while she dressed, warning me to stay away from the rooster. Like any curious four or five year old, I always explored the yard and kept myself pretty busy. On this day I didn't see the rooster around, but I did find an A-shaped ladder that had been left upright just behind our house. Of course I had to climb it to the top but was very careful not to dirty my dress. But, either the ladder became unstable and moved, or my foot not used to being shoed, slipped, and I tumbled through the ladder, about four or five feet down the middle, hitting my mouth on a step or on the ground. I still see myself running into the house dirty, bloody and crying loudly, scaring everyone around me. My mother ran to me, hugged me and asked,

"¿Que pasó mija, la tumbó el gallo?" Through my tears my brain was scrambling, and I clearly remember knowing that I couldn't say I'd climbed the ladder so I nodded my head yes, *"si, fue el gallo"*. From that experience I earned a chipped eye tooth that refused to fall out until I was almost eleven years old, constantly reminding me of that Arvin rooster. Many years passed before I confessed to my mother that I had been a *traviesa*, and the mean rooster on that occasion had been innocent.

I will forever have the scent, of fried onions and green *chiles*, in my nose and in my heart. Images of my mother standing in front of the stove are frozen in my brain. If she was in the house, it was to stand in front of the stove. She was always there, then she would disappear, leave for work then reappear, then she was gone again. Everything she did was accomplished with rapid motions, chopping potatoes, cooking *tortillas* and talking. Often as she cooked, she'd chat and laugh with the men, teasing them and they'd banter back and forth, enjoying her witticisms. Josefina was always at her side, moving in slow motion, placing *tortillas* on the table and removing empty dishes.

Apparently, as the story has been told to us, my father returned after about six months, and my mother took him in. What could he have thought? I believe he must have felt humiliated. Lola had succeeded without him. All the boarders, including Josefina, respected and revered her; she was *Señora* Lola to them. Financially she was secure and was in fact saving a lot of money for those times. He could see that she hadn't actually needed him. She had established a home and a pseudo business that she and Josefina managed well, working together as partners. I imagine she was in emotional agony so she put all her strength and energy into physical labor, and from this point on, her identity would always be defined by how much and how hard she could work. She could almost match Martín in strength, and she definitely outmatched him in endurance and perseverance.

Martín joined the household working alongside Lola, and in two years time, they bought a lot across town and had a modest new home built. We moved into it the spring before I was to start first grade. We had lived in *la casa de lamina* for three years, longer than in any house during the previous nine years. I missed it. It was the only home I could remember. My memories of Josefina were tied to that house, and she didn't move with us but instead returned to live with her brother. I had lost my confidante and companion, but school filled my time, and soon I must have forgotten her. Our life was good. My mother and father were a strong team and in love again.

ALBUQUERQUE

In 1964, the Peace Corps was still relatively unknown to the general American public. I can't remember how I came to be aware of it, but it surely wasn't because I was well informed or politically savvy. Most likely my desperation to get out of my hometown prompted me to investigate all alternatives and possibilities. I remember that I was searching for a space, a safe yet exciting geographic space where I might rightfully fit. There was also an interval in time that I wanted to preserve, to enlarge, a void that sought a consequence. Intuitively I knew it would happen. Either by chance or intelligent scheming, I happened upon an organization that accepted me and didn't make me feel out of place. I listened to the words of John F. Kennedy, and somehow, in my young psyche I developed a strong belief that I had something special to contribute to the less fortunate of other countries. Somehow I totally disregarded the fact that there were also poor people in the United States. But I must have felt like a very fortunate girl myself, one not in need of assistance. I've wondered where I appropriated that perspective.

It was only after I arrived at the University of New

Mexico in Albuquerque, that first night in the dorm, that I felt a sudden pang of fear and homesickness. As I settled into my bunk bed, with a stranger who spoke almost a foreign tongue sleeping in the bed below me, I questioned my decision of blindly leaving home and going God only knew where. I missed my mother. She prayed for me, cooked for me, made my lunches and washed my clothes. Who would watch over me, I wondered. But by the next morning, as I met the other volunteers, I was swept away with excitement and promptly forgot about my sheltered past and my boring little town. At least 98% of the volunteers in my group were college graduates, in fact, most had graduated just weeks before the training started, and only a handful of us had working experience but no college. Four of us were Mexican, as we called ourselves in those days, none of us had completed college, and I had only taken one college course at the local junior college. I was very proud and not at all surprised when all four of us passed the training and went on to spend two successful years in Brazil. At the end of the twelve-week training program, only 50% were selected to continue. Our group of 60 girls destined for Northeast Brazil was whittled down to 29, and I was one of the triumphant ones selected to fulfill what we all thought of as our patriotic duty.

It wasn't until many years later that I realized the Peace Corps was conceived as a weapon against the Cold War and was in actuality just meant to be anti-Communist propaganda. It was Kennedy's idea but not really his creation. This was left to Sargent Shriver, Kennedy's brother-in-law and the first director of the Peace Corps. He embraced Kennedy's political theme of a New Frontier and envisioned Peace Corps volunteers as pioneers of international development. It was the Kennedy image and mystique that shaped Peace Corps ideology and motivated thousands of young men, and young women like myself, to leave their homes and voyage to Third World countries. But it was Shriver's direction and leadership that molded the PC volunteer prototype. Peace Corps Washington, composed of great white men educated in America's elite universities, wanted the cream of American youth to become the pioneers of the New Frontier in foreign relations. Their ideal volunteer was middle-class, college educated, blond, blue-eyed, beautiful, robust and physically perfect, tough, individualistic, 20 to 22 years of age, and willing to become an emissary of American society. Volunteers from the early years of the Peace Corps were often called B.A. generalists or more frequently, just Kennedy's Kids. This referred to a type of person who could be trained for teaching or community development, and could do about anything non-technical and non-scientific. I always assumed it was my dental lab technician experience that got me into the Peace Corps, although it was a skill I was never called upon to use.

In our group, the three young Mexican women and I were an anomaly, to say the least. How we all got past the FBI investigation, the testing, the interviews, and the observations and scrutiny of the various selection boards still confounds me. Our group also had two African American women, both college graduates, but the all-male group training for Colombia had only one African American trainee. The application process that required the completion of a 12-page form, six personal references, a six hour exam, and a battery of medical tests was devised to ensure that only the privileged of American youth would be considered acceptable. Even though Peace Corps was based on liberal Democratic principles, ethnic minority volunteers were clearly absent. During one peak period of Peace Corps volunteerism, in 1968, there were approximately 8,000 volunteers in the field, and only 111 were African American, less than 1% of the total. Individuals from other ethnic groups, such as Mexican Americans, Asian Americans and

Rafaela G. Castro

Native Americans were too few to get an adequate count.

Yet, ironically, even though the four of us Mexican women might have been accepted as an administrative oversight, we were absolutely perfect for Peace Corps life. Our cultural heritage, language aptitude, social experiences, and the ability to work extremely hard prepared us well for the rigors of Peace Corps training and for life in South America. We were flexible, knew how to overcome hardships, were physically strong, had high expectations of ourselves, lacked self-indulgence, were definitely not complainers, and were used to a basic diet of grains and legumes. I have forgotten the backgrounds of the other women, except that they were all from California, but I know they must have experienced a few forms of negative social confrontations and personal setbacks in their young lives. We were always excited, high energy, and generally very pleased with ourselves. Carmelita was from San Francisco, and I do remember that while she was in Brazil her brother was in Vietnam. They both returned home about the same time in 1966.

We were accepted without question by most of the other volunteers, but East Coast and Midwest people weren't sure how to categorize us. I remember a humorous incident from our first backpacking adventure. The whole group was divided into small groups of eight to ten girls, each with a male leader, and the group I was in happened to have three of us Mexicans in it. I've since wondered if it was by accident or planned. Around the campfire that night our conversation somehow delved into the Mexican experience in the U.S, and a gentle New Jersey girl innocently stated, "I've never seen a Mexican." We all laughed good-naturedly and one of us said, "Well, you're looking at three right now!" She chuckled with embarrassment, unsuspecting that she would be irrationally selected out of the group. Even though she didn't become a Peace Corps volunteer she became one of my best friends and I've remained in contact with her for almost forty years.

Social scientists might conclude that I came from a disadvantaged socioeconomic background, but I didn't know that in the 1960s. I did come from a farm working family, although being the youngest I didn't work in the fields as much as my sisters, but it was a way of life that we never forgot. On our migratory trips to the Fresno vineyards, I was relegated to staying in camp with my grandmother, but if I begged enough sometimes my mother would take me with her to the fields, and I worked as her partner. While she cut and filled her bucket with clusters of grapes, I played with dirt clods under the 110-degree heat of the vineyards. Once her bucket was full, she'd dump the green grapes onto the large brown paper I'd laid out between the rows of vines, and it was my job to spread the grapes evenly, taking out the leaves and twigs so they could dry up into small shriveled raisins. I thought this work was more grown-up than helping my grandmother prepare dinner, outdoors under a canvas canopy, for thirty to forty people. When we lived in Arvin, everyone we knew worked in the fields. In the fall, once school started, during 'show and tell' time on Monday mornings, all the kids, Okies and Mexicans alike, bragged about the number of pounds of cotton they'd picked over the weekend. I never thought of my family as poor because we always had plenty of food to eat, but I always knew exactly what I could ask for and expect to receive from my parents.

Training was intensive and full, but there was still opportunity for commiserating about fatigue and hardships with enough time for sharing and bonding, and even romance. Surprisingly, to me, I made friends easily. In spite of the tight schedule and long hours, we managed to find time for beer and late night conversations. I had never lived away from home so it was a particularly remarkable experience for me to live in a college dormitory among white people. Today I can't remember exactly how I felt during those weeks, but the letters I wrote home reveal the sense of wonder and newness I experienced daily. My letters also betray my adolescence and naiveté. I was three years out of high school, had lived my whole life in farm working towns or small communities among Okie, Mexican, Italian, and Portuguese families. Thrown into an academic environment, introduced to physical activities like mountain climbing, repelling, trekking, and the then new Outward Bound program of survival training was exhilarating and thrilling for me. I never felt out of place and mistakenly or not thought I was just like everyone else. Many of us were from California, and I liked that I belonged to this group and felt pride in being from the state most represented among the volunteers; we felt a certain righteousness in fulfilling John F. Kennedy's vision of humanitarianism and altruism for our country.

Peace Corps training was the perfect adventure for me at that time in my life, and I reveled in it. I loved the challenges, the excitement and tension, the physical exertion required of me, the intellectual provocations, and the suspense of the future. I continually stunned myself as I conquered each strenuous hurdle. The course work was more boring than challenging, but I performed as well as my college graduate cohorts, and the Portuguese language classes came easily to me. In idealism, I was in the top group also, I was planning to save, teach, and aid every woman and child in northeast Brazil. I foolishly felt that I had an innate ability, a gift that the others did not have. I knew what deprivation was about, I thought, and what the concerns of poor women were. As it turned out, eventually I discovered that I had more in common with many of my Brazilian friends than with some of my Peace Corps comrades.

The letters I received from home encouraged me to eat well, rest adequately, not work too hard, go to Mass, recite the rosary, take my vitamins, and to return home if I didn't like the Peace Corps. Both Lola and Martín wrote me that they were very proud of me and advised me to behave well and not cause them any grave disappointment. I instinctively understood what they meant, but if I'd been asked to translate their concerns into details, I wouldn't have known exactly how to explain it. My mother kept urging me to reconsider, *pienselo bien* she'd say, about me going to Brazil. She didn't really believe I would go, and she constantly found hidden messages in the letters I wrote that confirmed to her that I was *disgustada*, unhappy, homesick, very tired, and probably too embarrassed to just return home. Her letters were always signed, *"Su mamá que la Quiere Mucho y no la Olvida, Dolores Castro."* I loved her letters but always doubted myself after I read them.

The selection process to determine who was or was not Peace Corps material was an intimidating psychological strain that constantly hung over us. Recent published books about Peace Corps training describe the reasoning behind the Selection Board procedures and how the process was intended to pick out the best young, typical American representative possible. An important consideration was supposedly to limit the number of incomplete service terms by screening out the atypical trainees. In the early years of Peace Corps, 15% of volunteers returned home before finishing in-country terms. The twelve-week training sessions had 'mid-boards' and 'final boards' convened to discuss every trainee in detail, to evaluate their answers to the many psychological tests, their performance in the classroom and on the hiking trails, and to look at personality and attitude traits. Psychiatrists played a dominant role in choosing the individuals that fit the profile of the ideal Peace Corps volunteer, the Kennedy-Shriver pioneer image. We never learned who was on these boards, but fear of de-selection was very real and an incessant topic of discussion among us. I always thought I projected my Mexican family values, yet here unknowingly and ironically, I was being molded into an ambassador of American culture and values.

That the world I came from was very different from that of most of the other *americano* volunteers was effectively thrust upon me when I returned home for ten days before leaving for Brazil. A boy, we were boys and girls then, actually a young man who'd become a good friend during training invited me out. He drove to my home in Rodeo to pick me up in a little red very expensive-looking Sunbeam. It was exactly like the one Elizabeth Taylor crashed in the movie Butterfield 8. He drove across the San Rafael Bridge saying we were going to a party at the home of one of his friends.

I tried not to show excitement as I rode in his cute expensive car, and I especially had to control myself when we pulled up in front of a lavish home somewhere in the hills of Marin County. I faked feeling cool and casual and concealed my pleasure at finding myself in such surroundings. The house was right out of a Rock Hudson-Doris Day movie; grand, streamlined, split-level, a fabulous 1950's home. It was early September and still warm. We wandered out to a patio and stood around a kidney-shaped swimming pool and soon had drinks in our hands.

My friend Jim introduced me around to his friends. I felt attractive enough wearing my best and only simple black, all-purpose dress that I had bought for New Year's Eve. Confident that I was appropriately dressed, I didn't feel totally out-of-place. The guys were polite, pleasant but didn't demonstrate any real friendliness or interest in me.

Jim had graduated from Cal the previous spring, and as a graduate, he was treated like the elder statesman. No one seemed curious about how he'd spent his summer, nor asked about his future plans. They were all intent on the task before them. This wasn't purely a social gathering; they had to decide which boys they would allow into their alliance, their fraternity. It was the end of rush week at the University of California, Berkeley and time to choose the distinguished lucky pledges.

Oh! I thought, I'm at a fraternity party, that's what this is. It could have been a cocktail party for a corporation's Board of Directors. The seriousness with which these twenty-plus year-old men set about to decide the future of their fraternity was similar, in my mind, to determining suitable business partners for a law firm or a bank merger.

The handsome young men were gorgeously dressed in what appeared to my inexperienced eye to be very expensive suits. They were healthy strong Anglo boys, prosperous, upper class, *"americanos ricos"* as we said in my family. I was awed by their self-confidence and poise. They circulated, mingled, conversing softly with each other as they solemnly discussed whom to exclude from their elite society.

There was a definite leader, a tall striking blonde man, who stood apart with his beautiful girlfriend but who didn't mingle. The others all came to him. Everyone swirled around him, talking to each other and then coming back to report to him. They weren't boisterous or ill behaved; in fact, they appeared consciously to not smile too much nor laugh too loud.

Of course there were also girls at this party, but somehow I can't recollect them as clearly as I do the guys. They mingled also, but mostly with each other, while the men roamed around consulting and debating. I was introduced to the leader, and his beautiful girlfriend, but they mostly made small talk about their summers. She had been in Europe and had just returned in time for the start of the semester.

Rafaela G. Castro

As the elder statesman, Jim was consulted about certain candidates. I remember he gave his opinion from time to time. I thought he stood out from the rest of the young men, perhaps he had matured during the summer, or maybe it was because I liked him. Or perhaps it was because his heart wasn't into fraternity affairs any longer - he didn't display much enthusiasm.

Despite being an outsider in so many ways, I was actually enjoying myself. I was fascinated by the dynamics of the negotiations, and I remember wondering, "Is this what college is about?" I always thought the college experience out of my reach, and I remembered how I often drove through Berkeley with my friends, enviously ogling the UC campus.

But on this night, I was feeling triumphant and somewhat kind-hearted. The ignorant rebuffs of the young men didn't faze me. Riding in the cute Sunbeam and socializing around a swimming pool in Marin County would have been a preposterous fantasy for me a few months earlier, but at this time in my life, I had something extraordinary happening to me, and I could hardly contain myself.

Once in a while a guy would come up to Jim and me, utter pleasantries and then look at me and ask, "What house do you belong to?" or "Which house are you from?" At first I couldn't understand the question. Being out of my realm, it took me some time before I realized that "house" meant "sorority house" and that they thought I was a sorority girl. I promptly explained that I wasn't in a sorority and that I didn't even go to college. I had to repeat this statement various times as different guys asked me, "Which house?"

Finally, I told one of them, "I don't belong to a house, I don't go to Cal, and I'm leaving for Brazil next week." Unimpressed, he walked away. I'll never know if Jim told his friends that he had spent that summer training for the Peace

Corps. We became friends primarily because we were both from California. Although during training everyone became friends with everyone. Jim was selected out at the end of the twelve-week program. I vaguely remember that he had been ill during part of the summer and possibly was selected out for that reason but I also remember that he was Jewish.

But I wasn't too concerned with his life because I was so absorbed with my own plans. The opportunity to live in Brazil for two years was the greatest thing that had happened to me in my young life. I knew it meant a major change for me but did not yet realize the impact it would have on my future. I was leaving an old way of life and rushing into a new one, unaware that I could never return. The social maneuvers of young university men didn't interest me; I was stepping into another world.

We didn't stay at the party very long. Jim had already left the fraternity business behind and had to look towards the future. That was the last time I saw him. We wrote to each other for a year or so. My letters from northeast Brazil described droughts, poverty, illnesses, and death, while his letters described protests and urban riots. He became a VISTA volunteer working on an American Indian reservation in Montana, and gradually we stopped writing. When I returned to California two years later, our society was so transformed that fraternity parties were considered politically unfashionable.

I've never forgotten that party and remember it as a dreamlike wistful silent film. I had observed a world that dealt with organized exclusivity and secrecy and was an enormous contrast to my own simple way of life. Years later, I thought of that fraternity party as the epitome of an age. I hadn't realized at the time that I had been a bystander to the end of an era. It was only a couple of weeks later that students, possibly even some who were at the party, at the University of California, Berkeley campus shocked our entire

Rafaela G. Castro

country with a piercing determined demand for their right to free speech. But when that event occurred, I was in Northeast Brazil in shock at the poverty I was witnessing there.

essay 4

LEAVING

We always called ourselves Mexicans when I was growing up, never Mexican American, or Chicano. *Nosotros los mejicanos esto…*, and *nosotros los mejicanos aquello….* It was a recurring motif in our dialogue as we discussed our comings and goings. In Arvin we went to school with white kids whose parents came to California during the dust bowl migration of the 1930s. They were called Okies, sometimes Arkies. There was no identity problem among us because we were mostly Okies and Mexicans. Oh, there was another class of people, the growers and business owners, but we didn't know who they were. We knew who we were, our language was distinct, we were proud, our identity was clearly visible on our surface.

We each had identities within our familial relationships that were intimately shared with our immediate families and with grandparents, uncles, aunts and cousins. But we also had communal identities that we displayed when we were in public together as a family, at church, shopping, or social functions. And of course we each had a third identity, the one we presented to the public culture as separate

Rafaela G. Castro

individuals, when we were in school sitting at our desks in the classroom, on the job, or out in town alone. This was the hardest identity to maintain because it required strong personal control and a healthy sense of self-confidence, qualities difficult to preserve when one is alone and isolated. Actually, it's rather admirable how as children we learned to maneuver our diverse individualities, depending on where we were, who we were with, and who we wanted to be. Our public and familial identities sometimes merged into our own brotherhood that was already private and had a special private language. *Nosotros los mejicanos*, an expression that actualized the togetherness we experienced and at the same time provided us strength and security. It bound us together while keeping us disconnected from the rest of society.

There were times when I felt my identity was fluid and could ebb and flow into the various cultures I encountered. It wasn't something I thought much about, it just seemed to happen. I could move between two languages and be private while in public by switching to my secret language. During my childhood I felt, unconsciously, that I was special, that it was a gift to have two languages, and even today I continue to feel this way. But it was more than just knowing two languages that made me feel distinct. I always felt there was a difference about us, our family, that caused me to feel positive about living. Perhaps it was just childhood. A child's world is small, enclosed, and happiness comes easily. There was a similar feeling about being Catholic. My mother often told us that only Catholics went to heaven so I knew I was special in that way too. In the early 1950s, we spoke of having a nationality, not an ethnicity. We would ask each other, "What is your nationality?" My nationality was Mexican, and I thought anyone with a dark olive complexion was also Mexican and could speak Spanish like me. If they weren't Mexican, they had to be Okie.

Spanish was the language of our home although I can

hardly remember not ever speaking English. My sisters and my many cousins, who started school several years before me must have taught me. We frequently spoke in both languages, but as the years passed, we switched completely to English though Spanish was still always spoken at home. Lola and Martín were fully bilingual, both born in the U.S., and they both learned to read and write in English and Spanish. Lola learned to read Spanish when her mother, my grandmother, enrolled her in a small private class taught by a local Mexican woman in Canutillo. I imagine it must have been somewhat of a sacrifice for a widow with six children to pay for Spanish language reading lessons. It was very important to Cipriana that her children learn to read Spanish. I remember how my grandmother loved to read, and she must have wanted to pass this passion on to her daughters. Even though she was only four years old when she crossed the border into El Paso and lived her entire life in the United States, she had tremendous pride in being Mexican. To be literate in her native Spanish language was fundamental to her. My parents never made a full shift to English and continued to speak to each other and to us only in Spanish. Interestingly, as they became older, their Spanish speaking capability evolved into a more complex cultural intercourse. As a middle-aged man, Martín returned to southern New Mexico and spent a lot of time in Juarez and Chihuahua where he reinvigorated his Mexican Spanish. And Lola, who for many years worked along side women from Mexico and South and Central America, learned to speak a Spanish infused with words and phrases that reflected other Latino worldly experiences. I disliked it when she spoke to me in English. She would become somebody else's mother in that language and was no longer mine. In her later years, whenever I called her, and she answered the telephone in English, I knew she had company and I would ask, "Who's there?" If she spoke English for too long a

period, she'd get tired and say, *"..se me cansa la lengua..."*
During all of my travels away from home, I'd write to her in
English, and she'd write to me in Spanish.

My entire life has been a perpetual struggle with
verbalization, with Spanish words and English words, with
speech in general. I've never felt that I fully mastered either
language and I've often experienced a choking feeling when
hundreds of tiny little letters and words become jumbled up
in my throat and keep me from exquisitely expressing
profound sentiments lodged in my mind. As a child I learned
to fight off this combative feeling towards language and
talked as rapidly and as much as I could to whoever would
listen to me. I loved to talk and was fortunate, or
unfortunate, depending on how one interprets it, to have
been cared for from the age of one to about six by a Mexican
woman who lovingly and patiently listened to every word I
uttered. Josefina, widowed and middle-aged, came to live
with us some months after I was born because she had no
place to live and to assist Lola, who worked in the fields
alongside Martín, keep house and care for her three small
daughters. Although in those years we were living a rather
indigent life, I think it was a mutually satisfying
arrangement, and Josefina grew to love Lola and helped her
survive through demanding and demoralizing times. She
devoted most of her time to watching over me, and I can
remember many hours of long extended conversations with
her. She didn't speak English, liked to read, and we regularly
saw her with books and periodicals as she sat in the kitchen.
One hand held her monocle while the other hand held a
newspaper or dish towel. I still don't know very much about
her background except that she was born in Mexico and
came to Arvin to live with her brother. She must have
received some formal education because the Spanish she
spoke was different from that of most of the Mexican
workers we knew. In *la casa de lamina*, bathing was a

complicated and lengthy affair for us because we had to fill a *tina*, a metal tub, with hot water so if Josefina didn't want to take a bath, she'd elegantly state, *"Mi cuerpo no me pide agua."* And we'd all giggle when in our language she clearly made a *pedo*, but she would explain it away by stating, *"Ay, se me salió el gas."* She was a slow moving, graciously patient woman who had few necessities and few pleasures.

I learned much of my Spanish from Josefina so consequently I was often reprimanded for speaking loudly and sounding too much like an adult. One of our rituals was for me to pretend that I was translating the newspaper comics to her, but now I can't remember which language I was pretending to translate. Regardless, she always gave me her undiminished attention, spoke to me as her equal, and bestowed upon me the conviction that at all times I had something very important to say. There were also several other adult Mexican men around our home at that time, *bracero* workers who came to our house for their meals, and they seemed to enjoy talking to me as much as I enjoyed talking to them. As a result, I became quite outspoken in both English and Spanish and developed a reputation for being *muy habladora*. My opinions were often dismissed by my mother with the exasperated comment, *"¡Como le gusta averiguar a ésta muchacha¡"* All my teachers from first to third grade wrote little comments on my report cards stating that I talked way too much in class. One also commented that one day I'd make a good citizen. I thought that was a great compliment, but by the fourth grade, I was being bluntly castigated for speaking too much Spanish, even on the playground.

While Martín was a man of few words, although they were often strong ones, Lola was chatty and rather witty so it's possible I inherited my affinity for long wordy explanations from her. A strong childhood memory I have embedded in my subconscious is that of Lola and her three sisters sitting around the kitchen table in one of their homes speaking in a tongue that sounded like gibberish to us children. They loved to *platicar* together for hours at a time and whenever they sat at a kitchen table, drinking coffee and smoking, lots of us kids would stand around, listening and hanging on to their words. We all understood Spanish and English, so if they wanted privacy to discuss an adult topic or to speak of their husbands, they had to switch to their own idiom. What they were speaking that sounded like an exotic language to us was a Spanish form of Pig Latin. They would look at each other, and one would make a statement, giggle, and then another one would answer, and in this way, they took turns speaking slowly and deliberately, conveying private messages to one another. "Nofo tenfegofo gafanasfa defe cofocifinarfa", and the response to this comment might be, "Dafalesfe pufurofo frifijofolesfe". *(No tengo ganas de cocinar.) (Dales puro frijoles.)* Their secret language bonded them more closely to one another, and to us children they appeared as one solid governing matriarchal body. As a child, I was fascinated by their womanly utterances and inflections, and it made an everlasting impression on me that my mother and aunts could speak a language all their own. This was another gift only available to our family that I tucked away into my 'special' mental pocket. It was an argot they learned as young girls living in Canutillo, twelve or so miles outside of El Paso. There is no well known name for this form of speech in Spanish, and years later, one of my aunts described it as, *hablar con la f*, because the ending added to each cluster of consonants is f, while in English Pig Latin it is ay. In Mexico, I have since learned, it is known as *el idioma de la f*. By the time I was a teenager, they no longer spoke this hidden language, but the concept of pleasurable indulgent dialogue and rhetorical social exchange, the art of being a *platicadora*, was already a cherished component of my character.

Lamentably my need to express myself never carried over into writing intriguing novels or short stories, but I did develop a propensity for writing letters. I've kept and cherished probably the first letter ever written to me, dated February of 1953, from an uncle who was in the Air Force. After we moved from Arvin to northern California when I was nine years old, I corresponded with many of my cousins and friends and still have several of their letters, full of terribly misspelled words, stashed away in my personal archives. These letters were all written in English since by then, it had become our primary language. I didn't learn to read and write in Spanish until I studied it in high school. Before joining the Peace Corps, I had been away from home by myself only twice, once to a one-week majorette and music camp at Lake Tahoe, and the second time on my two-week vacation to Hawaii. Of course each trip required that I write countless letters and postcards to my family and friends. In fact, I remember that during the seven days that I spent at Lake Tahoe, I wrote two letters to my high school boyfriend, and received only one from him, but upon my return home, his first comment to me was, "Why did you write to me so much?" Obviously he hadn't missed me as much as I had expected.

My mother, never believing that I would be accepted into the Peace Corps, was almost heartbroken as I prepared to leave. Even when she had reason to be happy, she always managed to maintain a melancholic expression on her face. She didn't seem to believe in happiness. Suffering was more interesting and rewarding to her. By suffering for her children, I still believe she thought she was ensuring herself a distinguished place in heaven. Even so, I remember how she organized a great going-away surprise party for me. She worked hard cleaning the house thoroughly and making special party food. Working hard keeping a clean home also ensured a place in heaven. My father played his records of

Mexican music, and everyone, both my friends and theirs danced until well past midnight. I still have pictures of this party, and there is one of my mother and me together. She is sitting in a large armchair, and I'm sitting next to her, squeezed into the small space left on the chair, but almost on top of her lap. Her arm is around me, and we are both laughing, but while I look into the camera, her head is turned, and she is looking directly and lovingly at me. I am very happy, and when I look at this snapshot, I can still remember the excitement I felt that night, still feel her loving gaze upon me. But at that moment, I was not wholly aware of Lola's sadness.

During the days before I left for New York, I noticed how she was extremely quiet and undemonstrative. I didn't ask questions or say anything, mostly because I was so agitated and busy, with lots of matters to attend to, things to do, shopping, packing, but I did wonder about it. Finally I asked my older sister if something was wrong. She told me Lola was feeling hurt because I was so happy that I was leaving. Naively I had expected her to be as excited as I was. Her unhappiness troubled me, made me feel guilty, but I had my bags packed and one foot out the door. I was already detached, and she knew it, and she never forgave me for it, never.

I loved my mother very much and wanted to share everything in my life with her. It was not often that I misinformed her or purposely kept secrets from her. When she was receptive to me and showed an enthusiastic interest, I communicated everything to her. She knew all my friends, all my boy friends, how much money I had, what I spent, how I felt, what hurt, everything! At some point, before I started on my adventure, I vowed that I'd write to her every week while I was in South America. In fact I usually wrote her twice a week, she saved most of my letters, and a few years after I returned, she presented them to me. I read them for the first time thirty-two years after I'd written them.

Reading and studying the hundred and twenty-plus letters that I wrote reveal to me a person that I never really knew. Who was that child, that girl full of confidence, optimism, strong opinions, and spiritual strength? Who was that young woman, I've wondered, who wrote these terribly corny letters? I didn't know her and still don't remember myself as I'm represented in these texts. My education and knowledge were very limited at that age, but I was positive of three things, I was a Mexican, a Catholic, and I was Lola's daughter. The letters are sensitive, somewhat insightful, loving, consoling, naïve, educational, guilt ridden, and at times sad. Yet they reveal the religious, moral, cultural, and ethical values of a young girl raised in the 1950s and 1960s in a Mexican working class home. I feel embarrassment as I read them, yet I know they reflect genuine sincerity at the time I wrote them.

Recently I read an observation about written correspondence by the mystery writer P.D. James, in her memoir *Time to be Earnest*, that provided me with a healthy perspective and an earnest respect for that young woman correspondent from Northeast Brazil. James states, "A letter is paradoxically the most revealing and the most deceptive of confessional revelations. We all have our inconsistencies, prejudices, irrationalities which, although strongly felt at the time, may be transitory. A letter captures the mood of the moment." (p.79) The letters I wrote to Lola were unmistakably confessional and truly captured the love and loyalty I felt for my mother during the years I was away. I tried to share my life with her, as if she were there with me, so I wouldn't be missed so much. I wrote a great deal, I wrote every night and turned myself inside out for her, in order to make her a part of my daily life. It is only now that I realize I've never learned how my letters were received at home.

For her part, my mother wrote me very warm and affectionate letters, revealing her love for me, and expressing her fears for my safety, sentiments she could never have stated to me verbally. After I returned home, we never discussed what we wrote in our letters to each other. Lola never conceded that I had once led a Brazilian life nor ever acknowledged the openness and candor of my letters, but for many many years afterwards, she continued to remind me of my transgression, when she'd start a sentence with *"Cuando me dejó y se fue para Brasil..."*

After spending two years in Brazil, I became a very different person, more grownup at least and different in simple obvious ways, but also altered in mysterious ways that even I couldn't exactly pinpoint. As my brother-in-law stated, "the Peace Corps ruined Rafie," meaning he didn't like the person I had become; but I liked her. However, my experiences made me irrevocable, there was no turning back, no returning to the small town I'd left behind, no blank acceptance of the behavior and values expected of me by family or friends. I couldn't acquiesce to the social and cultural life I saw around me among my sisters and friends. Once again I had to start a search for a space where I might fit.

Ironically, it was my capacity for acquiescence that made my life in Brazil feel so effortless and contented. Even today I can still say that those years in the Peace Corps and Brazil were some of the happiest of my entire life. The *americanos* complained about everything because, I guess, they came with expectations, of what I don't know. But I had no expectations and accepted every one and every situation as genuine and wonderful. The people, the food, the customs, the language, the Peace Corps staff; everything was fresh and marvelous. In my letters to my mother, I tried to convey my excitement and love for everything Brazilian with such expressive words as 'nice', 'great' and 'neat'. The young woman who returned to the United States two years later was no longer a wide-eyed adolescent, plain and unrefined. In that time I received an American and a Brazilian education, gained some intelligence, and acquired several worldly habits.

I learned to sleep in a hammock. I learned to drink beer. I learned to talk to strangers in Portuguese.

I learned to make travel arrangements to cross a continent and traveled alone fearlessly.

I learned to stay in a hotel alone.

I learned that I was an intelligent and committed person who could work alone. I planned projects, wrote lectures in Portuguese, and presented them to groups of students, adults, and rural poor people.

I traveled throughout Brazil and South America. I spent one night on the beach in Rio de Janeiro with a man I thought I loved, and on another night, I slept in the heights of Machu Picchu.

I had traveled alone through the jungles of the Amazon and stayed in a hotel in Manaus waiting for a freight plane to Colombia. I had been thrown into a tributary of the Amazon River with a 16-foot boa constrictor around my body, just to have my photograph taken.

I had experienced a unique cultural position in Brazil. I was a foreigner who could pass for Brazilian, which offered me a privileged status during my bus trips and country travels. I enjoyed the privacy of an outsider but did not appear to be the outsider since I didn't stand out in a crowd. No one stared at me as I walked the streets of Belém, Recife or Rio, yet once it was known I was an americana, I was treated with the disconcerting awe accorded all Americans. It was an in-between social space that I learned to love.

I also learned to love Brazil and my many Brazilians friends, and I found it unbelievable that they also loved me.

ME AND MY MOTHER

My namesake was my mother's madrina, her godmother, and also her first cousin, who had died many years before my birth. Her name was Rafaela, and she was called Rafie, which became my nickname too. From birth it was the only name I knew, and didn't realize it wasn't my bestowed baptismal name until I was an adolescent. My eldest sister was named Juana because she was born on St. John's day, and my aunt, Lola's younger sister, gave her the middle name of Elva. My father named my other sister Herlinda after a baby sister of his who had died at the age of two. I have a tiny photograph of my mother as a baby, taken the day of her baptism, where an attractive serene young woman, her *madrina* Rafaela, lovingly holds her upright. Although they were first cousins, she was many years older than Lola.

Rafaela was greatly loved and admired by everyone in the family and was apparently exceptionally bright and quite professional for her age. For many years she worked in the local drug store where she was sought after and consulted by the whole Spanish speaking community of Canutillo, Texas. Her life ended tragically while she was still a young woman when she died during childbirth of complications related to a tumor, long before my mother and father were married. The baby also died, and my mother and her sisters sadly mourned their deaths. It's possible this sorrowful event formed the basis of Lola's belief, frequently narrated to us, that all women who suffer the pains of childbirth and have the unexpected misfortune of dying are ensured entry into heaven. Once I learned the story of Rafaela, I felt I was somehow exceptional, and it affirmed my belief that I was destined for a special relationship with my mother.

Yet, in my earliest childhood memories, my mother is mostly absent. Her presence is felt as an ethereal spirit or a nurturing apparition, but intense images of her don't vividly materialize in my mind until I'm about six or seven years old. In our new home, after moving out of *la casa de lamina*, she continued to work long hours, and her attention was constantly drawn away from us children because there were always many other people in our lives and in our house. There were cousins, aunts, and needy women that were taken into our home for short periods of time. Quite often someone was sleeping on our couch, the living room floor or both. Once, for many months, we had a whole family, with five or six children, living in our back yard in a large tent. Together with other men, my father dug an outdoor toilet for them to use in the far back area of our property. It seems to me I heard the story that their house had burned down and they had no place to go. Previously a small one-room structure had been built at the other end of our backyard and one or two *braceros*, boarders from *la casa de lamina*, would live there on and off. I remember one late evening when my father hid two or three Mexican men under our house for several hours while la migra was searching the neighborhood. And every year during the blistering months of August and September Martín organized his company of workers, made up of family and friends, and they journeyed up the San Joaquin Valley to Selma and Fresno to pick grapes. Martín negotiated contracts with one Armenian grower and supplied workers for him for several successive years. Our connection to all of the people that surrounded us revolved around farm work, fieldwork, finding long term work, finding a place to live, and the myriad complex needs of poor people earning a living. Neither Lola nor Martín was especially out-going, but somehow they developed a reputation for being resourceful and helpful and were continually sought after for advice and assistance.

Lola was born in 1922 in Canutillo, a tiny community that in the mid 1920s had a population of 300, located twelve miles northwest of El Paso. She was the fourth child in a family of seven, and in her own words, *era muy traviesa*. Her sisters referred to her as *la loca*, because of her bountiful energy and mischievous character. She always looked for ways to tease others and entertain herself. If she was sent on an errand a couple of blocks away, she'd make a straight line to her target, walking right through neighbors' yards and even through their homes; she'd walk in a front door and out the back door on her way to her destination. Both her paternal and maternal grandmothers lived with them when she was young, and she often played pranks on them. One of them had a favorite small pet lamb that she cuddled and babied and my mother would dye the lamb green or pink, with food coloring, just to provoke her grandmother. They lived in a small adobe house without indoor plumbing and had a wood-burning stove, but Lola's memories of her childhood were cheerful and happy. Her mother's mother, Conrada, was a notable cook and had once earned a living cooking meals for miners in Silver City, New Mexico when my grandmother was a little girl. In Canutillo, she was frequently employed to cook for weddings, *jamaicas* and other community functions. My mother loved going with her grandmother to assist her and to just be around the crowds of people. The family's life changed dramatically when my grandfather, ill for several years with stomach cancer, died in 1935. Lola was thirteen and had to quit school to stay home and take care of only one grandmother by then, two younger sisters and one brother while her mother worked. Like those of many poor people, her childhood and teenage years were short lived; by the time she was seventeen, she was married and had a baby girl.

My memories of my mother are images of her in perpetual motion. In my childish mind I see her as a character in an old-time silent movie, twirling rapidly with jerky movements going from one room to another, or as the main actor in a video that is fast-forwarded. I don't remember that she ever relaxed, took an afternoon nap, sat in the swinging chair on our small porch, or just lingered over a cup of coffee in the kitchen. She could not stay still; she was washing clothes, ironing clothes, cleaning the house, cooking for someone, or getting dressed to go work in the packing sheds. When it was bedtime for us, she was still up completing a chore, and when we awoke she was already dressed making coffee, *tortillas y avena* for breakfast, or she had already left for work. Our home was regularly full of music, voices and laughter. Lola loved Mexican music and even a little Hank Williams; consequently the radio was always on, and there would be humorous chitchat with whoever was living with us at the time.

Her extraordinary and meticulous attitude toward everything she accomplished extended even to the way she dressed to work in the fields, forever an enigma to me. At a time when most women still had to wear dresses and skirts to do farm work Lola wore Levi 501® jeans, considered of course to be men's pants; and she wore her beloved boots. The boots were not heavy work boots, they had a small heel, were high form-fitting and came up to just a few inches below her knees She worn them under her Levi's pants' legs.

Over a tee shirt, she'd wear a long sleeved man's blue shirt, probably my father's, starched and pressed, and a scarf covered her hair under a large straw hat. Every part of her body was protected from the sun, dust and pesticides, and she never stepped out of the house without perfume, make-up, and bright red lipstick. Her work clothes were always fresh and clean, and with her dark glasses and gold *arracadas*, she was the epitome of glamour to a small Arvin girl. Apparently Martín had problems with her wearing pants, and he let her know it, but by this time in their marriage, she had earned certain rights that she wouldn't give up. Driving Martín's red pick-up truck to work, she was a trendsetter and a leader among the younger Mexican working-women of Arvin. And, most importantly, I think she was a happy person at this time in her life; she had respect, a busy life, and as far as we knew, Martín was loyal to her.

Looking back as an adult woman I realize that at some point in my very young life, I made an unconscious resolution to win attention and affection from my mother, no matter what it took. And I set out to do that. I knew she loved me, and I felt well cared for, but I had become accustomed to accolades and to having my every word heeded by Josefina and the *braceros*, and my mother did not fill the lonely void I must have felt at times. I say "must have felt" because by the time I was seven, I did spend many hours alone. My older sisters, close in age to each other, ignored me, and friends were not allowed to come and play. It is only now I can see that for many years, I diligently worked to get my mother to listen to me, to look at me and really see me. My sisters have often teased me saying I was Lola's favorite. I have always wanted to believe it, but reading over the many letters I've written her and reminiscing about our relationship from childhood to adulthood, I see that I labored awkwardly to earn that privileged position. Somewhere along the route to maturity, I determined that my life goal was to prove my love for her because I didn't think other people loved her sufficiently. Other people like all the ones she helped in life, and Martín who was loutish and demanding.

It has to be difficult and perplexing for a child to expend energy arduously seeking love and attention. Yet, I have mostly happy memories of those years when we lived in our new Arvin house before we moved to northern California, although there is a poignant incident sharply etched in my memory that still surfaces periodically. It is a memory that rekindles a melancholic loneliness in my childhood that I didn't know existed, and have only acknowledged its presence since I entered adulthood.

One sunny day when I was in the second grade, during a lull in my mother's work schedule when she did not have to leave our house at dawn, I decided I wanted her to walk me to school. Our school was just one block away, and I usually walked with my sisters, and I don't know why on this particular day they left me behind. The school grounds started within a block of our house, but my actual school building was another two or three blocks farther, and I reached it by walking across sports field and a large playground. Once I reached the corner of our block, I had to cross a slightly busy street to get onto the school grounds. In a rare moment for her, my mother was still in her *kimona* at 8:30 in the morning when I became insistent that she walk me to school. She was home and I was craving her attention. Suddenly it became extremely important that she accompany me at least to the end of the block. I wanted her to hold my hand and cross the street with me. I remember begging and her declining, probably because she wasn't yet dressed. Instead she walked me out the front door and to the end of the short yard and would go no further. As a last resort, I tried to extract a promise from her that she'd stand there and watch me until I got to the corner, crossed the street, and walked on towards the school buildings. She agreed, I think, but I don't know if she promised. So, I'd walk a few steps and then look back to make sure she was still there, then I'd go forward a few more steps before again looking back. When I reached the corner, she was still there watching me, then I crossed the street and took a few more steps. I took very small steps and must have taken at least fifteen minutes to get on the school grounds. I remember turning to check on her once more and catching a glimpse of her still standing there in her pink chenille bathrobe just before a school bus came down the street I'd just crossed obscuring my vision of her and our house. In the two or three seconds it took the bus to pass before my eyes, my mother went back into the house I presume, for when the bus had gone, so had she. Her disappearance from my sight produced such an overwhelming sorrow within me that even now the memory of that morning resurrects an enormous heartache for that little girl who wanted her mother to walk her to school. I burst into tears and walked the rest of the way to my classroom crying loudly, not understanding why I needed to cry. I cried for such a long time that even my teacher couldn't console me, and eventually I was relegated to the back of the room so I wouldn't disturb the other children. Eventually the tears ceased. Perhaps I felt better after the long cry, or perhaps I just learned to suppress my tears. There was little time for crying and feeling sorry for ourselves in our lives then, and I've never narrated this story to my sisters or anyone else in our family, yet the memory lingers.

Lola never cried, or if she did, I never saw her tears until the day I left for Brazil when she was already forty-two years old. She did not cry, and she also was not demonstratively affectionate towards us once we became young girls and young women, unlike Martín who for years insisted that we hug and kiss him goodbye and hello on a daily basis. We knew what was expected of us, and we faithfully complied, but my mother didn't pamper us, praise us, nor needlessly gush over us in any way. I guess some would describe her as stoic, but she was only raising us the same way her mother had raised her and her sisters. Our lives were restrictive and confined to our home, and as long as we adequately completed our chores, we were left alone to our comic books and radio programs. Frequently our relatives and friends commented on how quiet and obedient we were. Today we would be considered suppressed.

My mother didn't know how to teach and explain things to us directly, female things and other facts about the world. Instead she had a whole vocabulary of words in Spanish that indirectly conveyed the information she thought we should know. Of course she was not alone in this practice, all of her sisters and her mother communicated similarly. When they spoke to each other, they knew what they were saying, but we were usually at a loss. It was as if they functioned within two communication systems, one being semiotic where signs, gestures, and facial expressions supplemented their uttered words that were often euphemistic and curiously brief. Their second linguistic system was direct, very candid, exclamatory and almost brutally honest. *"¡Ay, que fea!"* and *"¡Ay que tonta!"* were not infrequent exclamations to our ears. As children, we bounced between these two patterns of conversation often not understanding exactly what we were told to do or not do.

When speaking of female bodily functions they used phrases like, *cosas de mujer* or *emfermedades de mujer*; expressions that encompassed the whole spectrum of female socialization, health and ailments. When a young girl started menstruating, she was suddenly a *señorita*, whatever that meant, and when a *señorita* lost her virginity, she was instantaneously a *señora*, regardless of her age. If a woman never married, she was forever a *señorita* regardless of her age. Menstruation and pregnancy were viewed as illnesses, and when a woman gave birth, *se alivió*, meaning that she was cured. During our monthly cycle, we *señoritas* were observed as *estan malas*, we were ailing. If a man took advantage of a young woman, it was said *que le hiso un daño*, and *una mujer mala* everyone knew was a prostitute. And if a couple eloped it was said that "he" *se la robó*, in other words the girl was considered kidnapped.

It was a traumatic event for me when I became a *señorita*, and "it" was never fully explained to me. "It" came over me at the very young age of nine years and ten months. I remember it distinctly because I fully believed I was being punished for my joys of childhood, and for disobeying my mother. In elementary school, specifically in third and fourth grades, I was a rambunctious kid that loved the schoolyard play structures, especially the traveling circular rings. I competed with another girl to see who could last the longest spinning around with one leg in a ring, hanging upside down. I was adept at having each leg in a separate ring, hanging upside down as the whole structure moved in a circle. Not all the girls could do this, and it didn't bother me that my underpants, my *calzones*, were exposed. But, my mother scolded me frequently; first, for showing my *chones*, which was very un-*señorita*-like, and second because I might hurt myself. *"Se va lastimar,"* she would say to me. At the time I thought I understood what she was saying, but later learned that I was totally wrong. She wasn't worried that I might fall down and break a leg, she worried that I might damage myself in another way, what with my legs stuck in two separate rings hanging upside down for the entire recess period. A bodily impairment could occur. I was forbidden to get on the rings and show off my *chones*, but I did it anyway although one of my sisters tattled on me sometimes saying, *"Amá,* Rafie was showing her *calzones* to everybody on the playground again."

Rafaela G. Castro

On a very warm night a few weeks after the start of my fifth grade school year, something woke me in the middle of the night – I don't remember exactly what it was – but once I was awake, I felt an unusual and distinct wetness between my legs. My sisters and I shared one regular size bed, and they were both sound asleep. I sleepily walked in the dark to the bathroom, thinking I was just perspiring, and was I shocked to find what I thought was a vast amount of blood on my underpants. A horrible dreadful fear took my breath away, my heart hurt from thumping rapidly and from realizing that I was in serious trouble. I had disobeyed my mother and injured myself. Clearly something had broken inside my body. Was it from hanging upside down? Did I pull a muscle, although I didn't know the word muscle at that time, or was God punishing me for disobeying my mother? That, I concluded was the correct answer. God was teaching me a lesson. I had broken one of the Ten Commandments! It must be the one about honoring thy mother and father. I had dishonored my mother by hanging upside down exposing my underwear for the world to see. Very quietly I changed underwear, washed my bloody *calzones* and used gobs of toilet paper to try and block my bleeding injury. I crawled back into bed dreading the punishment I surely would receive from my mother in the morning.

Scared to death, my only relief was prayer. I had made my First Communion a few years earlier and was well indoctrinated on the power of prayer so I decided to recite the rosary. I didn't have rosary beads in bed with me and had to use the fingers of both hands to keep accurate count of the prayers. My little girl body lay motionless between those of my two older sisters while I used one hand to keep track of the five Our Fathers and used both hands to count the ten Hail Marys, that I recited five times. I'm fairly certain I completed the whole rosary before falling back asleep. I told no one about the breakage in my body, but within two days, my mother found my awkwardly washed underpants in the bathroom and figured out what happened to me. She called me from our bedroom, with my eldest sister present and asked me if I was bleeding, or something to that effect, and in a panic I timidly acknowledged my misdeed. With an almost imperceptible mischievous smile on her face she provided the following information in no more than three sentences. She told me "it" would happen to me every four weeks, and would last five days, *se va enfermar por cinco días*, and that I was to use Kotex which she would buy. She also told me not to eat bananas during those days. My sister did not utter a word. What I recollect is total bafflement mixed with great relief – so I had not injured myself on the rings – but what was this monthly ritual about? Who said I had to go through this every four weeks? I didn't like it one bit. It had crept up me, and I hadn't even been warned. Unbeknownst to me I had become a *señorita*, and I resented that Lola knew about it all along and hadn't indirectly informed me.

It must have been extremely difficult for Lola and Martín to make the decision to leave Arvin and move to Rodeo, a small town in northern California. This was another major move, in a period of fourteen years that took them further away from their southwestern origins. Leaving the southern San Joaquin Valley and moving to the San Francisco Bay Area was like moving to another country. I've spoken with friends who've emigrated from Mexico and we have found many similarities in our innocent, growing up migration experiences. Even though it was only a three hundred-mile move, we felt like our old way of life was a thousand miles away. In our New World, not many individuals spoke Spanish even though there were plenty of brown skinned people around; instead they spoke Portuguese or Italian. The contrast was more difficult for

Lola than for anyone else in the family. She was 31 years old, and, for the first time in her life was leaving the camaraderie of her mother and sisters. We moved out of our Arvin house, small with only four rooms but it was our own and had a big yard, into a tiny apartment in an old ugly World War II housing project. In terms of comfort, it was a step backward, and we'd inadvertently joined the ranks of the town's outcast Project Kids, but it was an economic step forward for Martín with secure employment which he'd never known before. His cousin helped him get hired at the American Smelting and Refining Company located across the bay from Mare Island. For the first time in our lives, we had health insurance with regular medical check-ups, dental appointments, and we lived the life of a 1950s isolated nuclear family. Having lived all our lives encircled by a large extended family, with many relatives and friends, we were lonely in our new surroundings. We left behind two grandmothers, at least fifteen uncles and aunts and countless cousins. The adjustment was not easy, but it brought us closer as a family, and my mother was there for me every day. It was easier for me to capture her attention.

For a while, Lola lived the life of a typical housewife and mother in the Bayo Vista housing project. We went off to school, my father went to work and she stayed home alone in the 600 square foot apartment with no friends, no telephone, and no transportation. She could only clean the place so much, but with her vigorous energy level, she acquired new or renewed former household skills. From my grandmother she had learned to bake bread, *pan de levadura* they called it and we loved it freshly baked and in our school lunches. This was an all-day activity since our miniature stove had a tiny oven, but for a time, we had weekly fresh bread in place of *tortillas*. Living on one paycheck was not easy so she also learned to sew and on a Singer pedal machine made us cotton skirts that we'd wear over our heavily starched crinoline petticoats. Unable to bear slothfulness, she worked hard to keep busy, but it was still difficult for her and she fell into a depression, although in those days no one called it depression. It was a solitary life for her and the weather was often gloomy and chilly. It rained a lot more than we were used to. A saving factor was that my father worked a rotating schedule, changing every three weeks. For three weeks he had the day shift, then swing shift and then the graveyard shift. He could be home with her regularly and they'd go off and explore the surrounding areas, or he'd sleep, and she could use the car. I quickly accommodated myself to my new school, made friends and was into my own childish world, but I do remember hearing bits of sentences like, *"Lola está muy nerviosa,"* or "nervous breakdown", and *"me estoy volviendo loca aquí."*

My grandmother came often by Greyhound bus to stay with us for two or three weeks at a time, and Lola who was very close to her would get ecstatic and be exceptionally attentive to her. The rest of us loved having her with us too. Her presence changed the dynamics of our family interplay and livened up our bleak days. All of my aunts were very devoted to their mother, Cipriana. She was literally a super woman who could do anything and everything. She'd sit down and sew ten pairs of pajamas for ten of her grandchildren or pastel cotton Easter dresses for several of us girls, all in a matter of a few hours. Sometimes on a Sunday morning she'd rise at 4:00 or 5:00 am to bake and frost three gorgeous fluffy two-layer cakes to sell at San Clemente Mission in the *La Loma barrio* of Bakersfield. She lived permanently with her youngest married daughter, and in their back yard she had a full chicken coop with many chickens that she'd kill herself on special occasions. Of course she also gardened and grew beautiful colorful roses that she'd place on the altar of San Clemente on Sundays. When Martín organized his farm worker troops for Fresno and Selma, Cipriana was the cook for the whole company of twenty to thirty people. Months before the trip she'd plan and await eagerly, constantly questioning my father, "¿Bueno Martín, cuando nos vamos?" She wielded a strong Catholic control over her grown daughters, and they all dreaded any disapproving glance from her. Even after they themselves were grandmothers, she'd frown if they had more than one alcoholic drink in her presence. We all loved to have her visit us, she made Lola happy, and she baked wonderful cakes and breads and narrated great stories. Even Martín loved her to visit us because of her great cooking and her affection and respect for him. Even so I would eventually feel overly anxious, waiting for her to leave because she was taking my mother away from me. When she was around, Lola only had time for her, and I selfishly felt neglected. As much as I loved my grandmother, I was jealous of her and can remember feeling happy, yet melancholic, when she returned to her home, for then my mother could return to me. Afterwards I would try to cheer Lola up and take the place of her mother by narrating silly stories about my friends at school. I was a talker, and my mother silently listened to me as she moved about the small apartment.

After completing a three-year penance living in the Bayo Vista housing project, we were able to move into a brand new tract home along the outer edge of Rodeo. Lola and Martín decided to permanently stay in Rodeo and they sold our sad little house in Arvin. Our new home had three bedrooms and two bathrooms, and my mother and father had a large bedroom with their own bath. I shared a small room with my sister Linda, and for the first time in our lives we each had our own bed. We moved into this, to us, a mansion when I started the eighth grade in a school that was just up the street. I think I can say that the years in this "new house", were probably my happiest and they lasted through my high school years and a bit later. My mother was working steadily now. She had started out with seasonal work in the canneries in Martinez, and then someone introduced her to See's Candies in San Bruno, a factory located over an hour's drive from our home. For many years she did seasonal work there, but eventually it became steady and evolved into permanent employment with union benefits. She loved the job and took great pride in her work, but her day started at 4:00 a.m. It was difficult physical labor, and she spent over two hours on the freeway commuting both ways. Her steady income helped the household, and we all must have felt that we'd come a long way from Arvin. No more farm labor or packing shed work during the summers for Lola and her girls.

Sometimes my mother took trips to Bakersfield to visit her mother and sisters, but she rarely stayed longer than a week or so. We all got along fine without her since we were well trained on running a household, but her absence felt as if the center column that upheld our home was missing. The atmosphere in the house was different, cold, tasteless, and we all moved about like sad zombies. I used to miss her terribly when she wasn't home, surely more than my sisters, and I used to go into her closet to smell her scent and feel her presence. It was a small walk-in closet, and was like a little house to me. If I walked in and stood in the middle, I could catch the fragrances of her wool dresses and coat. The shoes, boxes, and other closet stuff were well organized and neatly placed, and my father's shirts were starched and ironed, and all her clothes were very clean. Everything about her always seemed very clean. But her clothes still smelled of her and by standing in her closet and closing my eyes, I could breathe in her aroma and feel comforted in my loneliness. I was not a little girl when I experienced these bouts of yearning for my mother. I was already in high school, but still felt such despondency when I was away from her.

Our high school was small, made up mostly of kids from

Rafaela G. Castro

working class families, and my years there were full and cheerful. For one stressful year my sisters and I were all in high school together. While my eldest sister ignored me, she was the popular one, my other sister protected me from the arrogant upper classmen and class women; she hung out with a small group of marginalized Mexican kids and always kept an eye out for me. I was an average student and didn't exert myself academically, concentrating mostly on social relationships and playful activities with my girl friends. My friends' fathers worked at the C&H Sugar factory, the Smelting & Refining Company, or the Hercules Powder Company, and only a few had working mothers. We were all acutely conscious of our own nationality and boasted a provincial patriotism toward our motherland although none of us had ever been out of the U.S. Well, our family had been to Tijuana and Juarez but I didn't consider these cities out of the U.S. I was a cheerleader, a majorette, a student class officer and considered myself part of the "in" crowd in my class, although it was not the scholastic "in" crowd. There were few school sports for girls in those days, but I participated in GAA (Girls Athletic Association) after-school activities and even earned a sweater and a letter. I think Lola enjoyed our high school years. She was young enough, still in her late 30s, to understand the perplexities and traumas of being a teenager. We went to football games, dances, school trips, and she shared a detached interest in our friends. I had a steady boyfriend in my junior year, an Italian-Mexican boy that was well liked by both Lola and Martín. He was an important figure in my life for many years until I went to Brazil and left him behind along with everything from my early years. My grades were less than great even though I was taking college preparatory courses, for I was not thinking beyond high school; attaining a college education did not enter into my worldview.

My self-centered teenage years were marred by one

family episode that seemed to come out of nowhere, but remained quite vivid in my mind until adulthood when I was able to make sense of it. It was September. I was thirteen and within a few days would be starting high school. I was excited and scared at the same time, not really wanting to grow up and be in school with older teenagers. High school juniors and seniors were then referred to as "upper classmen," and in my eyes they resembled characters in a novel, grown-up and attractive. I was dreading high school and had a lot of thoughts going through my mind. My mother came into our bedroom very early one morning wanting to talk to us. We had relatives visiting at the time, and my older sister had given up her bedroom to our company and was sleeping with me in my bed. In an odd moment for her, my mother slipped into the other twin bed with my sister as if she just planned to visit with us for a while, but in a commanding voice she said she had something important to tell us. I thought it might be gossip about my aunt who was sleeping in the other room. Instead she said she'd asked our father to leave the house because she found out he was seeing a former girlfriend of his. My normally cheerful world turned icy cold. My body couldn't move from under the covers of my bed. I wanted to think of school and what I was going to wear on the first day. I didn't want to know scary things about the confusing world of adults. We all stayed silent and numb, not knowing what to say. Later that day my mother packed my father's clothes. We saw the suitcases, but I can't remember if he actually moved out of the house. My sister tells me he left for several days or maybe even a couple of weeks. Why can't I remember? Our relatives returned to Bakersfield, and a day or two later my father came and told the three of us he wanted to talk to us, something he'd never done before. We were teenagers so none of us talked to him very much. He took us for a drive down to the marina area of Rodeo and parked the car in a semi-secluded spot. How he was able to say these words I'll never know, but he told us he loved Lola very much, and he didn't want to leave. *"Yo quiero mucho a su mamá."* He asked us to talk to her and tell her we wanted him to stay. It was a scene out of a *telenovela*, intense and dramatic. Again none of us said a word. We didn't know how to talk about feelings like anger or love. In little tiny voices we each said "o.k." We didn't speak to my mother, at least I didn't, instead I ignored them both, and the crisis seemed to pass, never acknowledged openly among ourselves. I promptly made myself forget, but the memory stubbornly stayed, and several years later it was to come back to plague us.

My high school years were typical. I never or rarely behaved inappropriately for a young girl of that era nor committed any illegal acts. I wasn't interested in beer but did learn to smoke cigarettes when I was seventeen and maintained the bad habit for twenty-five years although I kept it a secret from my mother for at least five of those years. She left us pretty much alone to make our own decisions and mistakes without nagging or preaching very much. She loved clothes and appearances were important to her. She wanted us to wear clean clothes and look if not fashionable, at least presentable. If she didn't approve of our attire she would brashly let us know, *"esa blusa esta muy arrugada, quítesela."* Our clothes had to be sharply pressed, and our hair well combed, *"¡Ay que greñuda está!"* It was rare that we received a compliment from her. I remember only one.

Ever since our Arvin days when there had been a parade down Bear Mountain Street and I saw a skinny majorette toss her baton high up in the sky, I had wanted to be like her. At our high school, the majorettes, six of them plus the head majorette, were smart and popular, wore respectable costumes, short white corduroy skirts and long-sleeved red corduroy shirts, and as such had coveted positions. Try-outs were held each spring, and only one or two girls were chosen depending on the number graduating and leaving that year. Our music teacher, the bandleader made the selections, and his criteria were stately marchers and worthy band members. He wasn't looking for fluff or future fashion models. I practiced the regal marching step for hours and hours, and it paid off when Mr. Wigell selected me in my sophomore year. That summer, with money earned from my job at the Rio Theater, I paid a seamstress to make my uniform. My first marching performance was in the Sugar City Festival parade down Main Street in Rodeo before school was to start in September. I was nervous and remember leaving our house very early in the morning, wearing my brand new white boots, white skirt with little red shorts underneath, and my bright red military style corduroy shirt. The house was dark and silent as everyone was still asleep, but just when I was going out the front door, my mother sleepily walked out of her bedroom and saw me. I felt and looked taller than her in my marching boots. She stared at me awhile, smiled and said in English, "You look pretty, *mija*." For a moment she was not my mother at all, and the incident sits playfully in my psyche like a lovely little doll, because she'd never told me I was pretty before. If she ever caught me admiring my reflection in a mirror she'd comment that I was being *"muy volada"*, and she'd add something like, *"y apoco se creé muy bonita."* I suppose she feared we'd think too much of ourselves. We were always careful to show modesty and humility. My years as a majorette and a band member made my high school years especially memorable, and to this day, I maintain contact with friends from those years.

We had an unspoken, mysterious linguistic custom in our family, on the maternal side, regarding the use of the Spanish pronouns *tú* and *usted*. While adults usually address each other with the familiar *tú*, connoting intimacy and equality, the usted, implying reverence and respect is reserved for unequal relationships, people in authority such as teachers, clergy, and older persons. In some traditional families, children and parents use the more formal *usted* with each other. Often children are addressed as *usted* until they grow up when they are transitioned into the familiar *tú* class, that has been saved for peers and equals. In our family, the youngest continued to be addressed as *usted* even into adulthood. My grandmother Cipriana spoke to her youngest daughter as *usted* as did everyone else in the family while the other sisters used the familiar *tú* with each other. Lola spoke to my elder sisters as *tú* but reserved the *usted* for me, which she used all my life. I grew up totally unaware of these differences in how I was spoken to, but I knew there was a nebulous tender *sentimiento* between my mother and myself. While the use of *usted* implies respect, social formality, and is the converse of premature social intimacy, I was always *usted* and was placed at an obvious distance from my sisters. My *"usted"* was an acknowledgment that I was the youngest and disengaged from the rest of the family, yet not quite fully grown up. A strong sense of duty was implicit in her address and while treating me with respect, Lola did anticipate a certain obedience from me. Even as she scolded me, a profound formality was imbedded in her statements, *"usted se creé muy buena como que no nececita mi ayuda."* Now I believe she had a formidable fear of my growing independence.

When I graduated from high school, my mother had a special party for our close friends, just as she had for my sisters before me. Several of our cousins had dropped out before completing high school so Lola and Martín were intensely proud of us. We had reached an educational milestone in our lives. The next turning point could only be marriage. They wanted good clean office jobs for us so we could contribute to the finances of the household, and be able to enjoy ourselves before reaching that second sacred milestone. From my little part-time job at the Rio Theater, I saved money to attend a dental assistant school. Why? It was clean work, and I thought I'd like wearing a white uniform. But I was not destined to be a working girl for years and years as I waited for Marriage to arrive on a golden chariot so I could commence my true calling. Instead the Peace Corps called to me, and when I left home, my mother's and my relationship experienced a renaissance. It became intense and intimate through our letters, but then her life with my father started to unravel and deteriorate, and our devotion to each other suffered a transformation.

No longer needing the attention or guardianship of my mother as I entered my 20s, I was maturely prepared to leave home when I did. It felt so right for me to join the Peace Corps, and I had so many exciting and extraordinary experiences that of course I felt excessive guilt. It was such an unbelievable shock for me to learn I could be happy away from my mother. I felt I'd committed an immense ungrateful betrayal. She did not want me to go, telling me she worried for my safety, but I know she just wanted me by her side, as I had wanted her by my side throughout my childhood. It was many years before I dared to express even to myself the thought that once I was grown-up and ready to go out into the world, she wanted to hold me back. I couldn't comprehend it. Shouldn't all parents want their children to grow up and go out into the world? When she should have turned to my father, her husband, for support she turned to her daughters instead especially me, the unmarried one.

For two years, I wrote twice a week; long, five, six and eight page letters, double-sided, divulging my new life to my parents, never questioning if they were interested in what I was doing or with whom I was doing it. They wanted me to eat well, pray a lot, go to church, and tell them I was suffering and how homesick I was. They didn't want to acknowledge that I had a new life with friends from another world. But I wanted everyone to know that I was loved in Brazil as well as at home, and there was no need to worry about me. While I established a life for myself in my little town of Catolé do Rocha in the interior of the state of Paraíba, made friends with the parish priest, Frei Marcelino, and set a course of work for the mission I hoped to accomplish, the family life I idealized and left back home was literally coming apart. The perfect love I had thought Martín and Lola had for each other, their years of teamwork in keeping our family shielded from the evils of the outside world, their house that finally appeared to be the home of their dreams, everything that was important to them they were completely destroying. And this was happening only two years after we'd celebrated their twenty-fifth wedding anniversary.

I received gossip and nasty bits of information in the letters from my sisters and from both of my parents. Martín became less and less discreet in his philandering, unbeknownst to me an activity he'd been enjoying since my birth. He was seeing a particular woman who made malicious telephone calls to my sister's and mother's homes. Unwilling to accept it any longer, Lola moved out of our home and into the apartment of my by then divorced sister and her little daughter. I couldn't believe that my nurturing, Made-in-America perfect Mexican family was committing such social transgressions. Separation? Divorce? In my limited warm secure mind, these things happened only to bad people, people who didn't love each other, not to my model Catholic family. Where was God during their crisis? My grandmother and mother prayed to God every day, and where was He now? Every week I received letter after letter with painfully ugly accounts of offensive escapades and lies. I became a therapist and a judge for everyone in the family, and they all felt they needed to tell me who did what to whom, providing me with all the ghastly details. I didn't want to know but couldn't get away from them, and the letters kept coming. In one letter my mother clearly told me, *"Ay hija no quiero mortificarla con mis penas pero con platicarle descanso un poco."* It became my duty to listen and act as a surrogate minister for her. I felt awful, and suffered for her. I felt sorry for her and also somehow felt at fault for the problems in her life. Nobody ever said to me that I had broken up the family, but it just happened to disintegrate after I left my home.

As many of us may remember, there were disturbing and horrible events occurring in the United States during this period of time; the Vietnam War, racial riots in Detroit, Washington, Los Angeles and other cities. The innocent world I had known and left behind was an illusion, and I felt lucky to have escaped just in the nick of time from what appeared to be a huge unreliable crumbling structure. In the *sertão* of northeastern Brazil I felt safe, sheltered from the deceits of American life, far away from political disappointments, civic disturbances and social revolutions.

What a heavy burden, I, still a young girl, must have carried on my inexperienced shoulders. In many letters during my last few months in Brazil, I expressed fear in returning home and defensively described who I'd become. "Ma, I'm really afraid that I'm going to disappoint you when I come home. I can't tell you what to expect because I don't know in what ways I've changed. I only know that I have changed. Or maybe you won't even notice any change at all, I don't know, I just don't want you to be too disappointed." (May 8, 1966) I didn't know what was expected of me, but I instinctively felt that Lola was basing her happiness upon my return, and I felt too young to be responsible for such a heavy task. If someone had informed me that it was my duty to work and support my mother for the rest of her life, I would have lovingly accepted it as my responsibility. Of course I'd take care of my mother. But I suspected that what she wanted was my physical being and my soul. Somehow my presence would magically return our lives to the life we'd known before, in 1963, before my sisters got married and before Martín's latest extramarital affair, and before I had grown up and gone away. Lola wanted to return to the past and pretend that I'd never been to Brazil, had never been happy in another place, another time.

Eventually I returned home and was received as the Prodigal Daughter who had been away, lost, and had now returned to the home of her mother. Another party was held for me where my high school girlfriends came with their new babies. But unlike the Prodigal Son who returned to his father's house because he had no place to turn, I returned home out of a sense of obligation. I had no place to turn because it was inconceivable to me that there existed sufficient courage in the world to disobey my mother. I had the opportunity to extend my Peace Corps time in Brazil for one year and fleetingly considered it, but knowing it meant torture for my mother, I declined. In April of 1966 I wrote, "Ma, I am going to tell you the truth, that I am scared to return home. I am going to return happy, excited, and everyone there is bitter, sad and depressed. I don't know how I am going to take it. You have to understand that it's going to be hard for me, you'll have to be patient with me."

For most of my life I had been in pursuit of my mother's love and approval, and now I had more than was necessary for a young woman. After all my years of soliciting her attention, at the age of 22 I had finally earned it, unfortunately when I most wanted to be autonomous. Upon returning from Brazil, I enrolled at a local community college and worked part time in the office of an architect. Lola deluged me with her attentiveness. She had taught us to take care of our own clothes, clean the house, and since I was six years old, I had taken my turn washing the dinner dishes. Now I relinquished all household duties and she did it all, as if I was a man, a son. Only other Mexican women will understand how surreal this was for me.

Lola and I lived together alone in a one-bedroom apartment for seven months. She left my father in our house by himself. She packed up some household goods, some furniture, kitchen appliances, and set up a home for us in a town ten miles outside of Rodeo. She was determined that I live with her and give her life purpose. In October of 1965 she had written me, "*...nomas le pido a Dios que cuando vuelva a Rodeo no eche menos la casa. Nomas acuerdese que en esa casa me quise morir de tresteza por su ausencia, ni me quiero ni acordar.*" Because of my absence, she almost died of sadness. During those months I did try to be a companion and a dutiful daughter, but I was just barely keeping myself above water dealing with the culture shock, the hippie scene in the Bay Area, and being dumped by my Peace Corps boyfriend. The following summer I told my mother that I was moving to Berkeley to live with a friend, a good friend that she knew and approved of, but I couldn't explain to her why I needed this. Without discussion, she accepted my decision, but she never forgot it, and many years later it would unexpectedly be brought to my attention.

Lola loved new beginnings, new looks, and fresh starts. Her living room furniture was rearranged regularly along with her kitchen cupboards and linen closets. She could move from one household to another, and in a matter of days her new home looked lived in and comfortable. Her whole life was composed of new beginnings. While her sisters lived in the same house for thirty or forty years, Lola moved living quarters nine times in thirty years. She loved the mobile home where she lived, for twenty years, while she worked in the candy factory. It was the longest period of her entire life that she lived in one home.

While I made clandestine plans to move to Berkeley, she was sort-of courting Martín. During the time we lived alone she would disappear during the evenings while I was studying. It turned out she was visiting my father while they planned a new life together. They sold our Rodeo home and bought a house in Richmond that they painted and decorated together. Lola didn't want to continue living in the house where she'd suffered so much. It was the start of a new life for them, after almost two years of intermittent betrayals, separations, and finally reconciliation. Meanwhile I led the student life living in Berkeley but visited with them weekly. We, my sisters and I, were relieved they were together again and believed they were happy.

For the next few years, our lives and everybody else's in the country were in psychological turmoil. After spending two years in the Peace Corps, I concluded that I could probably handle college, and eventually became a student at the University of California Berkeley during the years of major student protests and strikes. There was no graduation ceremony for me or anyone else in 1970 because of the turbulence associated with the Vietnam War and the invasion of Cambodia, a cataclysmic event that almost put a complete stop to all academic endeavors across the country. The same month that I received a college degree in English, I embraced that sacred milestone; Marriage.

I'd reached the formidable door at the end of the colorful corridor that had no exit. There was no place to turn, no escape route. I married because I had to, it was what women did. It went along with plucking our eyebrows, wearing high heels, shaving our legs, and having unplanned pregnancies. In retrospect I can say I felt pressured, but was it self-imposed pressure? After all I was a child of the 1950s and already believed I'd evaded marriage long enough. I couldn't hold out any longer. What would my family and friends think of me? By the time I married most of my high school friends already had two and three children. But I was particularly concerned about my mother's opinion. I was taking trips with the boy/man I was dating, camping and other intimate outings. It was clear what was going on, yet I pretended it was all very monastic. Like many women, I married because I thought I was getting old, because I thought I had no choice, because I thought it was the quintessential event in a woman's life, and most importantly because I thought it would make my mother happy. A few years later it became clear to me that I had been wrong.

LETTERS FROM THE PRETTIEST GIRL IN ARVIN

As I've read and re-read the letters I wrote my family, it has dawned on me that I matured through my writing during the years that I was away. But what exactly does it mean to 'mature'? Does it mean to really know and comprehend oneself? That surely takes a lifetime. Or does it mean that one learns to step outside of oneself and become a witness to one's own insignificance in relation to the rest of the world? Or does it suggest that one has reached a stage in life when one becomes easily disillusioned with the ways of the world and the people nearby? Does it mean that one finally learns to judge and act on personal beliefs and values? If all this is true, then I did grow up while writing and receiving letters from friends and family while I lived in Brazil. I learned to concentrate and focus, to describe my experiences, to express opinions about my experiences, and to share those thoughts with friends and with my parents. I received many letters from relatives, friends, and friends of friends, asking me questions about my work and life. I became a reporter, sending news back to the homeland, about my adventures and escapades. Today I have in my possession only those letters I wrote to my sisters and mother and father. They not only chronicle my adventures in Brazil, but the actual writing, the taking of pen to paper, the mental exertion of constructing descriptive sentences, and the unveiling of my most private thoughts, brought about a coming-of-age enlightenment. My letters were like writing assignments, my homework and my education. Living in Brazil was definitely an education, but it was an anticipated cultural growth, while writing was like a qualifying exam. I explored my inner world and developed the means to articulate what I found within myself. It was an unexpected reward while in pursuit of my *gran provocación*.

My first letters from Albuquerque and Peace Corps training were purely descriptive, informing my parents of my busy life and schedule. By including my mother and father in my daily activities, like hiking, horseback riding, and the practical training, I thought they'd feel safe and secure about my well being. My letters had a light tone and I tried to make funny observations for their entertainment. They didn't ask questions nor make comments about my experiences, but I was later informed that they enjoyed my letters. For instance, my father got a big kick out of the fact that I had to buy boots for the overnight treks into the Sandia Mountains. He loved that I was in possession of a pair of high-top boots. I wrote hastily, not taking time to express self-doubts, serious thoughts or provide fine details.

June 12, 1964
Dear Ma and Dad,
My roommate's name is Carolyn. She's from Atlanta, Georgia, and just graduated from college. She's real nice and talks with a Southern drawl, so I'll probably be talking like a Southerner when I come home.

July 8, 1964
We had lots of fun last weekend on our hike. The bus took us to the foot of the mountains, and at 3:30 p.m. we started walking up. Each of us had a pack that weighed between 30 and 40 pounds. That was the hardest part, carrying that pack. We were in small groups and camped out in different places. My group camped out the highest, it was about 2 1/2 miles up and it took us almost 2 hours to walk up. We camped in a beautiful spot and could see all of Albuquerque from it. But that walk up was hard. It was hot and carrying all that weight and walking almost straight up! For a while I was afraid I couldn't make it, but I surprised myself and was one of the first ones up there. (I was third.) The next day we had to rappel again, this time from a real high steep mountain. Then we walked back down the mountain and had a steak fry and watermelon at the bottom. We got home at 8:00. I was so tired and my face was all burned, but I had a good time.

Of course I didn't go to church that Sunday, but at the Newman Center they distribute Communion every day at 5:45 p.m. for the Peace Corps trainees. I've been going to Communion every day. There isn't time for Mass because we get out of class at 5:20 and they stop serving dinner at 6:15 and we usually have a class at 7:00. But it's nice to receive Communion every day. About 6 or 8 of us go. We say one decade of the rosary together, for everybody in the Peace Corps. There are quite a few Catholics here.

July 26, 1964
We got two more shots last week, which makes 11 shots that we've gotten so far. We all have scars. Somebody said we were getting 15 but I think we're going to get more. They don't seem to want to stop giving them to us. Every Tuesday, Bang! Bang! two shots just like that! The Selection Board meets Tuesday and we should know by that night who is selected out. So think of me that night.

August 13, 1964
You were right, in my last letter I was tired, but not unhappy. Well, you can imagine how I felt after getting up at 5:15 all week. This week we went to a different place every day. Yesterday we made home visits with a Visiting Nurse. My nurse had mostly old patients. She had to give bed baths and shots, to two old ladies. Most of the homes we went to were Mexican homes. I really enjoyed that. Tomorrow we go to Santa Fe again to a Catholic Maternity Institute.

Ma, the selection board meets in about two weeks and I don't know what's going to happen. Since the last de-selection two more girls have left to get married. Anyway, if I get selected out I'll be home a week early, if I make it I'll be home September 5th. No matter when it is, it'll be soon.

August 31, 1964
Well, now I'm so excited I don't know what I'm doing! We're going to leave for Brazil from New York on September 17th at 9:00 p.m. But I'd like to arrive in New York on the 16th to visit a girl that was selected out.

My mother wrote back that she'd shared my letters with some of my high school friends that had visited her. That pleased me since I was having fun and wanted everyone to know about my bold adventures. I was caught up in a formidable exercise and didn't question anything, not even the de-selection process.

I loved Brazil and Brazilians from the very first day when I stepped off the plane in Recife. Feeling exhausted from the long plane ride, I remember also feeling apprehensive and overwhelmed. I looked at everything through the eyes of a dazed child wandering in a candy store. Yet I approached my new life with an open mind and an open heart. Like a sponge I absorbed the exciting colorful sights, boisterous sounds, tropical aromas and the graciously friendly people. It was a challenge to convey my complex emotions to my family.

September 18, 1964
I don't know how to describe Recife. It's a very old city and it has two canals that run right through the center. It's fun to walk across the bridges. The streets are very narrow and there are people everywhere. It's like Mexico, you know, everybody likes to sell things, stands and open shops everywhere. Some of the buildings look like they need a paint job. They're yellow and the paint is peeling. But they're building new modern buildings everywhere. You can see a nice new building going up between two old rusty ones.

The strangest thing about being here is that nobody around can speak English! It seems so funny that everyone speaks Portuguese and a lot of the people look like average Americans. I think I'm really going to like it here. I can't believe how lucky I am.

Rafaela G. Castro

Gradually my perceptions of what I was observing and experiencing became discriminating and I had to express my opinions in writing. Since we were trained to be health workers, to assist in public health posts, and visit homes as *visitadoras*, we were immediately conscious of the sanitation and nutritional conditions of the women and children. Culture shock set in very quickly once we witnessed the horrendous poverty of the rural communities of northeast Brazil. For weeks I was in a joyful state of titillation, fluctuating between shock at the impoverishment, and the excitement of accepting my new country and my home for the next year and nine months. My initial flush of euphoric adoration melted into realism and I started looking at everything, including my PC colleagues' conduct, with a critical eye.

September 22, 1964
Tonight I'm in João Pessoa, the capital of the state Paraíba. You wouldn't believe how different this city is from Recife, it has some nice and pretty areas but most of it is bad. The poor areas are really bad. No paved roads, they're all muddy and full of holes and little, tiny houses. Little kids running around with no clothes on and big full stomachs, which is a sign of malnutrition. It's really sad but I hope I can live in an area like this. I've liked everyone that I've met.

September 24, 1964,
Here in João Pessoa we've been visiting hospitals and clinics. I can understand quite a bit now, but when a doctor starts talking about diseases and medicine it's pretty hard. I am disappointed that I don't understand more than I do.

Some kids are having trouble with the discomforts. There is so much complaining. The bathrooms are bad and dirty. In fact I would prefer an outdoor bathroom. The showers aren't too bad, the water barely makes a dribble and of course there is no hot water. Some of the girls have already been sick with diarrhea. But nothing has bothered me, I've been fine. I know I'll get sick, everybody always does. All they serve us is beans, rice and bread. Sometimes meat, and always coffee. The coffee is good. For breakfast, we always have café, and different kinds of bread and biscuits, sometimes fruit. I love the café. In the morning we have café with hot milk, but only in the morning do you have milk with your coffee. After dinner you have a tiny cup of a very very strong coffee, called cafézinho, and you put a lot of sugar in it. It's great.

The Brazilians are wonderful warm people. They love to look at us. They come in our room and stand around and we can't get rid of them. But when they start to speak, I can't understand them. It's frustrating. All the babies I've seen are just beautiful. And it's funny how many people mistake me for a Brazilian that is until I speak. They say I have the features of a Brazilian, not of a Mexican, but I think a lot of the people here look like Mexicans

I haven't yet asked myself "what am I doing here." And I'm hoping I never do, but I'm really disappointed in the way our girls are acting. They're complaining about everything, and it's just the way they told us it would be. But don't worry about me because so far I like it.

Rafaela G. Castro

As I progressed and adapted to the Brazilian culture and made friends, I narrated my daily exploits in my letters home. Following the example of the other volunteers I also wrote in a journal. Between my letters and the journal I judiciously wrote down all the meticulous details of my daily routine. We completed a six-week in-country service training where we lived with other PC volunteers so it was a comfortable gradual immersion into the language and culture of the country. We were in temporary living quarters, dependent on each other, and at first held back from making close friends with community people, but it was a period of rapid learning and tremendous growth.

September 28, 1964
Today was our first day of training at the hospital. We had a few lectures, of course in Portuguese. I understand much better now. We saw two deliveries too. The people around here are so poor. You wouldn't believe the houses or shacks that surround this town. A lot of women have their babies at home but the doctors try to make them come to the hospital for their first baby. One lady walked into the hospital with her baby hanging halfway out! The baby was not upside down, with the head coming first, instead the feet were out and the head was stuck inside. The woman had a midwife with her, but the midwife didn't know what to do since the baby was like that (breech). Anyway, when the nurse had the baby out I thought it was dead. It was all purple and it wasn't breathing. She massaged it for awhile and finally it started to breathe. It was so exciting to hear it cry. We saw another woman have her 12th child. The people here are so poor!

It was mid-November before we were finally sent to our permanent sites. Now, I thought, my true Peace Corps experience will begin. But, I was mistaken. I was assigned to a large city, Campina Grande, and invited by a middle-class doctor to live with him, his wife and their five children. They lived in a large house almost in the center of the city. Another PC volunteer assigned to the city lived nearby, also with a family. I was disappointed because I had wanted to live in the *sertão*, the dry desolate backlands, in a small interior village. Yet, Dr. Mello welcomed me warmly, treated me like a daughter, and I soon learned to love him and his family.

Because it was a large city, it was difficult for Judy, the other volunteer, and me to penetrate the bureaucracy of the complex health department. In frustration, we'd frequently end our days by visiting an American missionary family that lived in the city. There were two wonderful and friendly families that took us in and often fed us delicious American home cooked meals, but their presence spoiled my image of a true, rough-and-vigorous Peace Corps adventure. Campina Grande was a transportation hub, where all the buses from the interior and the coast connected. Consequently, we were constantly entertaining PC visitors from all over the state. I had envisioned myself isolated, deep in the interior, away from urban culture and American influences. It didn't occur to me to ask for a transfer, but unexpectedly I was urged by another volunteer, who was stationed alone, to join him in a small town in the interior of Paraíba. After weeks of waiting for approval from our regional director I was finally allowed to go to Catolé do Rocha, ten to twelve bus hours away. Immediately I fell in love with the *sertão*, the town, the people, and the convent where I lived for over a year.

Rafaela G. Castro

February 1, 1965
Dear Ma,
*I've finally arrived here in my little town, Catolé do
Rocha. I'm pretty far from the coast, but I love it.
This is a real pretty town. It's starting to rain now, so
everything in the sertão is turning green. I love the
colégio, the nuns are just wonderful.*

*I went to the health post today and boy, is it in bad
condition! We have lots of work to do. Catolé has a
population of about 5,000. But the health post is
hidden and far from the poor areas. We're going to
try and move it to an empty building in the center of
town. Ma, the post is absolutely empty. It has one
chair and a table. The people go there and the doctor
(if he's there) writes out a prescription, and the
people go home. They haven't got any money for
medicine, so they throw the prescription away, and
the child gets well or dies, most die. There is no place
where the poor people can get help. I want to start a
young mothers club there. I'm so excited because I
have so much I can do, and I have such a good
working partner.*

March 9, 1965
*The other day, a woman came with a little girl, and
she got to the post after the doctor had left, and she
started crying. Ma, if you could see this poverty, you
wouldn't believe it. I visit the houses every morning,
these people are poorer than poor. But the doctors
and the people from the town don't care too much.
You should be grateful for all the benefits you have
in the States. Social Security and you have a hospital
plan. These people live from day to day and they*

barely make it. Little kids die by the tens, of dysentery. The people from one bairro are beginning to know me. I'm going to start holding health classes for young girls in a lady's sala.

Now, I thought, my real Peace Corps work is starting, and I immersed myself in the health and medical services of the community. My PC partner Terry was a great guy and we worked well together on some programs but he traveled frequently so mostly I worked alone. My idealism was quickly shattered because nothing was easy and no one cared if I taught just one English class once a week, sat in a vacant health post reading magazines, or lounged in a hammock all day. I thought up various ideas, all related to health, nutrition, sanitation, and I started project after project. Eventually I developed a loose program that worked for me and for the neighborhoods, *bairros*, that most accepted me. I started clubs for young women, the non-educated washerwomen of Catolé who spent their days at the creek, and gave talks on sanitation, personal hygiene, prenatal information, and general women's health. I translated English materials into Portuguese and had prepared lectures on various topics related to bacterial diseases, sanitation and the causes of the high infant mortality rate in the region. Families had ten and twelve children, expecting that half would die of *doença de infância*. I would travel to small rural settlements, sharecroppers' homes called *sitios*, and gave talks on safe water and the importance of constructing toilets. Periodically we'd dispense medication that we received from the state health department, such as drugs for worms, dysentery, and vaccinations for polio and typhoid fever.

Rafaela G. Castro

March 26, 1965
I got pretty discouraged this week. Two of the babies
I was visiting died of diarrhea. Everybody has
diarrhea here. Tomorrow I'm going to a school that's
nearby, to give a class on safe water. I met the
director when I was in Souza and he wants me to
come out every Saturday. It's a school for boys out in
the country, so I'm looking forward to it. Monday,
I'm going to give the same talk to some women in the
bairro. Everybody here gets sick from the water.

I made dear friends with many young women in town
and felt totally at home in mud shacks and in the convent
with the nuns and novices. I shared a bedroom with a lay
school teacher from the convent. Every night she wrote her
lessons while I wrote hundreds of letters, on onion skin
paper, to my mother, sisters, friends, and other PC volunteers
in Paraíba, Brazil and even Colombia. I wrote my mother
about my double life, stating "I have two worlds almost. My
social world of the town itself, which is one group, and my
working and social relations with the poor people of the
bairros, that is an entirely different group." I led an external
social life with my Brazilian girlfriends, my on-going projects
and in my relationships with some older adults in the
community. But I also had a blossoming interior life, a life of
the mind. The Peace Corps provided each site a book locker,
with a couple hundred paperback classics, and I had it in my
bedroom. It must have been the first time in my life that I
was conscious of developing my mind, so to speak, by
reading and writing. My outer world, full of laughter,
sharing food, singing, and passing on essential health
information was in Portuguese while my inner world carried
on an English monologue with my mother and grappled
with the disgrace of my disintegrating family in California.

I loved my Brazilian life even though I never became fully integrated into the upper echelons of Catolé's society. My work with the poor people stigmatized me as an agitator and possibly a communist. Even so, gradually I became happier and happier and felt more secure in Brazil than in the previous life I'd led in the U.S. As the months speedily melted away, I worried that I wasn't fully contributing to the mission of the Peace Corps and wondered if I would actually accomplish my goals and fulfill my pristine dreams.

September 16, 1965
Dear Ma,
I don't know if you remembered, but it was a year ago today, that I left home. It doesn't seem possible. And Saturday it'll be one year since I arrived in Brazil. I still don't know the language very well, I still don't know the people very well, I still don't know the customs or ideas of this country. Our time here is so short, what can we possibly give these people? They have given me so much in one year, much more than I could possibly give them in two. God has been good to me, I am exactly the same now, as when I left home, physically anyway. I hope I've matured a little, and I think some of my ideas and impressions have changed. I've come into contact with so many beautiful things and people that they must have left an imprint on me. But don't worry Ma, I hope (and should) be a much better person when I come home, than I was when I left. The Peace Corps did you a favor.

I met many amazing and memorable people that have stayed with me through the years, but a few became more than memories, they've become long distance permanent friends. One such person was the priest from Catolé do Rocha, Frei Marcelino. A Capuchin Frey, he was an extraordinary character, short and skinny, fair skinned, with blue eyes closely set in a large head. When I met him I thought he looked much older than his thirty-six years. But growing up in an impoverished northeast Brazilin household had given him a gaunt appearance. He was not handsome, but he had a wit and an infectious laugh. When he walked down the street a crowd of women, children, and dogs followed, appealing for his *benção*. With a huge ego, bordering on arrogance, he possessed a bottomless well of physical energy and incontestable determination. Nothing ever appeared impossible to him as his mind only saw opportunities and the bright side of every situation. His brown wool cassock flapped rapidly behind him as he rushed to attack with equal fervor problems caused by destructive forces of nature or destructive politicians. He could have been a distant relative of Saul Alinsky. At first I felt intimidated by him, but eventually we became best of friends and I often wrote about him in my letters home.

February 1, 1965
The padre here is Frei Marcelino, I haven't met him yet because he's in Recife right now. But he's a little bomb, he's flying around here doing everything. Guess why he's in Recife? Castello Branco, President of Brasil, was in Recife Saturday, for about four hours, and Frei Marcelino was there to talk to him about electricity for Catolé. And he talked to him too! Can you believe it? This little padre talked to the President of Brasil about getting lights for a town of 5,000!! That little Frei can do anything! Right now we have electricity from a generator from 5-11 p.m. But there's a huge waterfall in Pernambuco that

supplies energy to most of the Northeast, so he's trying to get power from there.

March 9, 1965
Frei Marcelino is finding us a place to move the health post, and he has all kinds of American drugs that he got I don't know where. He built a school with money he got from Germany. He can do anything! Right now I'm writing by candlelight, we haven't had electricity for three nights.

May 30, 1965
We're starting a big polio vaccination campaign June 1st. The vaccine had to be kept on ice so it was flown in by plane. I had to stick around the colegio all day waiting for the man that was bringing it. At 12:30 pm, I heard the plane fly overhead, so I hurried and put on my clothes, and 2 minutes later Frei Marcelino was here for me. And off we flew to the field where the plane landed. Me and the boy scouts!! Frei M. likes to do everything big, the scouts played their drums and we made a lot of racket coming into town. We're going to vaccinate for two days, and have enough for 6,000 kids. There are at least 10 cases of polio in Catolé already. We need the vaccine!

September 16, 1965
Tonight we have real light! Finally the electricity was hooked up. Everyone went wild, and Monday we're going to have a big inauguration festa. It's real bright and it's full time, 24 hours a day, instead of 5!! The whole town has to thank Frei Marcelino for this.

Through the past years, Frei Marcelino made several trips to the U.S. and visited my home twice. I've also returned to Brazil twice to see him and I think of him as my family. When he first came to see me, I lived in Rodeo soon after I'd returned from Brazil. He tried to lure me back to Catolé do Rocha by saying, "You don't belong here. I can see it in your eyes. Come back to Brazil with me." Feeling closer to him than my family, I was tempted because Lola and Martín were separated at the time, and home was not a happy place. Marcelino's life took many interesting turns and he's now in a place I never could have anticipated. From Catolé he tried to get elected as a state assemblyman representing the interior region. He did not win, but months after the election when the elected man died unexpectedly Marcelino was appointed to the position. He settled in João Pessoa, the capital of the state, as he served out his term. Later he worked for the state, and earned a Ph.D. in education from the University of Paraíba where he also taught. Eventually he also earned a law degree. As he worked as a floating priest, unattached to a specific parish, he dabbled in all kinds of political activity. He once told me the Church was the perfect setting from which he could best advance his social and political objectives. But he also had personal aspirations. He was in his mid sixties when he left the Capuchin order and married a woman who'd patiently been waiting for him for many years. Today he refers to himself as a "married priest" and not an "ex-priest" because he believes the Catholic Church will eventually change its position on this question, and because in his mind he can only think of himself as a priest.

The many times when I doubted myself and wondered if I was succeeding or accomplishing anything, I'd unburden myself in the letters I wrote my mother. I don't quite understand it, but I expressed feelings to her that I couldn't express to anyone else. Even though I frequently shared my escapades with other PC volunteers, and we joked about our successes and failures, I can't remember confiding my insecurities and doubts to anyone. Yet with my mother it was as if I were confessing to her, possibly awaiting an absolution, so I could feel cleansed of my dark shadows and uncertainties. Fearful of feeling alone in the world, I could always connect and feel close to her through letters across the thousands of miles.

Sept. 9, 1965
Today, everything is settling back to normal, after a week of festas. Yesterday was the end of the 8-day festa for Catolé's patron saint. For 8 days there has been a sort of bazaar down by the church. Also the day before yesterday, was Brazil's Independence Day, so that day was full of bands playing, kids singing, reciting poems, and everybody marching. We had two holidays in a row, this week is going to have 3 weekends! Things are almost normal, but we still have campaigning for the gubernatorial elections. And campaigning in Brazil is one big party! Every night there are bands playing, girls dancing Carnival in the streets, and lots of speech making. This is going on until October 3!!

Because of all these festas, my work has been a little slow. I'm working at the health post every morning, but my afternoons have been pretty free. My first English class is tomorrow night; Saturday I start the Health class at the Escola Agricola; next week I start teaching a First Aid class at Frei Marcelino's school. My club had a meeting today, we didn't get much done, but we decided to have hot dogs at our next meeting! It was their idea, not mine.

Rafaela G. Castro

I think we're going to have electricity full time by September 15. There was a big party for all the workers today, at the school. It's going to be great. Poor Frey Marcelino worked so hard for that. He is really a good guy, and I like him a lot, but we argue and fight like cats and dogs. But I know he likes it, and you know I like it too.

November 6, 1965
This week I finished my First Aid classes, and yesterday my students gave me a little festa. They were so nice! They sang songs, and made speeches. One girl wrote a poem for me. They gave me a present, a beautiful sewing box, made from special wood, the kind I've sent home. I know that some people here like me, but I don't really know how they feel or think about me. These girls showed me that they accept me for what I am, and that they almost understand why I am here.

At times I feel like I am working so alone. I work because I push myself. Nobody really cares if I work or not, except myself. But these girls showed me that my work isn't unnoticed. They know what I'm doing and they almost understand why. That should leave an impression on them, when I leave.

November 11, 1965
Last week I wrote you about a program my First Aid students gave me. Well, last Monday the girls from my prenatal classes gave me a party and they gave me a photograph album with my name on the cover. Really I feel so bad afterwards. I am so unworthy of their gratitude. I've hardly done anything here. Now, I am just hoping I can leave a little impression, an

impression of what I represented. And the only way I can do that is by having more contact with the people. So I think I am going to move out of the colégio, and find a place in one of the bairros. I love it here, but I am not making any sacrifices at all, and I have such a short time left, I have to try and do more.

I've wondered if my passing from advanced adolescence into adulthood didn't originate with the news that my parents' marriage and the family home I'd known were disintegrating. In fact, my father was having an affair, and I heard about it from each of my sisters and my mother. My mother asked for my opinion, or was it my advice? I resented receiving this information, but as a dutiful daughter, I naively felt obligated to assist somehow. So I prayed and wrote them long letters full of advice and admonishments. Our written exchanges became an intimate façade, a delicate precarious word bridge, full of phrases that could never have crossed our lips face to face.

October 7, 1965
Ma, I explained how I felt in my last letter. I hope you can understand it. From your letter, and the way you talk about my Dad, I'm sure that you still love him, and I know that he still loves you. I wish you two would get together, forget that you have any daughters, and only think of each other. Ma, I know you want me to decide what you should do, then years later you can say that you did what I wanted. But I'm not going to tell you what I think you should do. I'm going to wait for you and my Dad to tell me what you're going to do. Ma, don't forget, you're the parent, I'm the daughter. You shouldn't center or plan your life around me. I can fit in any place. I'm

being honest with you. I think it's wrong that you rely on me so much. How can I decide something that is going to affect your happiness for the rest of your life? Only you can do that. I'll close for now, don't forget that I love you.

January 16, 1966
Ma, you ask me how I'll feel if I return home and find you and my Dad separated. I don't know. But I think I would rather have you separated than living together and hating each other. Yet, at times I do dread returning home, but that is understandable, isn't it? You're all going to have to be patient with me and my reactions. My excitement in coming home, and then finding everything different; it's going to be difficult.

In spite of distressing messages from home, I was still able to experience fascinating vacation trips and even romance while in Brazil, which I shared in my letters as well. Peace Corps granted us vacation time and in the first year I traveled throughout Brazil with two PC friends. Since our flight had landed in Recife, we hadn't seen the southern part of the country so we traveled by bus all the way down to Saõ Paulo, stopping in Bahia, Ouro Preto, Belo Horizonte, and Brasilia. Our trip ended with several days in Rio de Janeiro where we fell in love with the Copacabana and Ipanema beaches. Exhausted we flew back to Recife where we each resumed our dedicated work schedules. My second year, I courageously decided to venture across northern South America to visit a PC volunteer in Colombia. I had fallen in love with him when we'd trained together in Albuquerque, and we had met briefly while in Rio de Janeiro. The story of that relationship belongs in another manuscript, but my journey through the Amazon region to meet him in Bogotá was like a spectacular precursor scene to an Indiana Jones movie. Not wanting to travel through the southern part of Brazil again, I chose to fly over the Amazon River to Manaus, and from there to Leticia, a jungle town in Colombia that borders Brazil and Peru. From Leticia, I caught a military freighter plane that flew me to Bogotá. Because of the low passenger demand, the whole trip required a wait of two and three days for flights, at various points, on both legs of the trip. It was not a problem for me because I met fascinating characters and friendly people in every city. Traveling alone was a new experience that I thoroughly enjoyed. Wherever I stayed, I felt and was treated like a celebrity.

March 29, 1966
Dear Ma,
Right now I am in Leticia. The plane for Bogotá leaves at 1:00 pm. Up to now my trip has been just great. I have been traveling through a part of South America that is just fascinating. Last Friday at 6:00 am I took the plane for Manaus. It was a long trip and the plane didn't even make it to Manaus. I had to spend the night in Belém, the capital of Maranhão, which is right at the mouth of the Amazon River. I did a little sightseeing, but I had to get up at 4:30 am to catch the plane for Manaus, which is 1,000 miles up the Amazon River. It's not really a very large city, and there are thousands of Indians around there. I arrived about 3:00 pm and had that afternoon and all the next day for sightseeing. I am enjoying traveling alone, it is so easy to meet people. Yesterday, at 7:00 am I left for Leticia. I met a German guy who is traveling around South America and we have become good friends. Also on the plane there were 2 Columbian PCVs

returning from their vacation and 2 other Peruvian men and we have all become good friends. We are all staying at the same hotel. (Run by an American! The hotel is full of them!!) We are all going to Bogotá today. I am having so much fun with my Spanish. I don't even know if I'm speaking Portuguese or Spanish. It is so exciting to be in a different country. Don't worry, I am fine.

April 11, 1966
It is Monday now and you won't believe what I've been doing. Leticia is in the jungle and the Amazon River flows through here. While flying here from Bogatá I met an American who is a Vice-Consul for the U.S. in Colombia. He came to spend a week with an American who lives here and catches wild animals, (monkeys, alligators, snakes etc.) for a zoo he has in Florida. Mr. West (the Vice-Consul) introduced me to Mike Tsalickis, and Mike is the most wonderful person I have ever met. He has lived here 13 years and he takes tourists hunting into the jungle, and he insisted that I stay in his house. Yesterday he took me to the river and put a 100 lb., 16-foot, snake on me to take my picture. We went to visit an Indian village down the river too. Today we flew 2 hours in a Beaver (plane), walked an hour and a half into the jungle to visit some Indians that don't wear clothes, so Mike could take their pictures. Mr. West paid for the trip and he invited me along. Tomorrow they're going on a 3-day boat trip, hunting, and they tried to talk me into going with them. I would love to but already I've taken more than 15 days vacation. Tomorrow my flight leaves at 9:00 am for Manaus and Thursday I leave for Recife. I already have an excursion planned (into the jungle)

in Manaus, for Wednesday. This is unbelievable! The things I've been doing and seeing are things from the movies; they don't happen in real life. This is one vacation I'll never forget!

Mike Tsalickis and I corresponded when I returned to Brazil and even from the U.S. I received Christmas cards from him, but inevitably after several years I lost contact with him. His name surfaced some thirty years later when I found a newspaper article about him reporting that he'd been arrested for smuggling drugs into the U.S. Allegedly his illicit activities were connected to the Colombian drug cartel. It upset me greatly because I had looked upon him as a trailblazer and courageous frontiersman. I am again in communication with him, through letters, and he emphatically states he is innocent. He has been in prison in Florida for over seventeen years and is now in his mid-seventies.

Within a few weeks after I returned from this excursion, it was time to pack up my stuff and sadly leave my little town of Catolé do Rocha. Our PC group met in Rio for a de-briefing conference and from there I traveled around South America with a group of volunteers. It was a wonderful time for us as we ended a major personal commitment and looked forward to new endeavors in our young lives. We spent time in Argentina, Chile, Bolivia and Peru. I ended my trip in Mexico City, spending a week there, not wanting to return to California or to my home. In one letter I had written that, "I am still happy here, I love Brazil. I love the life. I am going to have trouble adjusting to American life. I think I worry too much about what I am going to do when I return." It was with regret that I boarded the flight home, after postponing it once, prolonging my stay in Mexico.

My transition back into family life was occupied with melancholic rituals. I was a witness to the dissolution of my parents' relationship. I had grown up by being their confessor, and they had become my children. I scolded them, consoled them, advised them and tried to get away from them. I knew I wasn't responsible for their failed marriage, yet I felt responsible, and was thus thrust into the role of ministering to their grief. They did come together again, one last time, for a couple of years. But it wasn't meant to be. They separated permanently and my father returned to New Mexico.

It was a difficult time in America's social history and I struggled to behave consistently with my coming-of-age consciousness. After enrolling in a local community college, I transferred to UC Berkeley graduating in the midst of tremendous campus turmoil.

essay 7

THE ROMANCE OF LOLA AND MARTÍN

They met as teenagers; the dark handsome slim boy with beautiful white teeth, and the homely, shapely, witty girl with horn-rimmed glasses and slightly buck-teeth. Was it love at first sight? He had a reputation with the girls; she'd never had a boyfriend. Even though they both came from poverty, they represented different economic segments of their provincial society. They were two *mejicanos* from the fringes of an agrarian social order. Their rural upbringing and their geographic proximity to Mexico, shaped their cultural identities. Martín was born and had lived all of his young life in a tiny pastoral hamlet five miles from Lola's town of Canutillo. In contrast to Martín's La Union, Canutillo, had a bustling population of about 400 people in the 1930s. La Union, twelve miles from the Mexican border, and historically known as *Los Amoles*, was one of the original missions on the famous Chihuahua Santa Fe Trail. This was the route Diego De Vargas took as he re-entered New Mexico in 1692, twelve years after The Great Pueblo Revolt. Other pueblo missions along the trail were San Miguel, La Mesa, and Chamberino where my grandmother,

Enriqueta, Martín's mother, was born in 1903.

In Canutillo, Lola and her sisters would frequently catch the train to El Paso to window shop and keep up with the fashions of the 1930s. They worked seasonally in the local canneries and had a small amount of extra money to spend on clothes. To Martín, Lola was worldly, sophisticated, and exemplified the 'other' side of their pastoral isolated existence. Martín had only reached the sixth grade. At the age of fourteen, he'd hitchhiked to California, and by his sixteenth year he already had a reputation as, *un andariego*, and an experienced seducer of virtuous girls. Lola must have known his history, but she dated him anyway. There were many prettier girls. Why did Martin pick her? Within a year, they courted, so-to-speak, got pregnant, married, and had a baby girl. Lola was a sixteen-year-old bride and a seventeen-year-old mother.

Like many people who grow up in poverty, Martín was afflicted with an innate belief in hard work and a commitment to family, but he had a weak sense of social discipline that he camouflaged with a large dose of arrogance. He learned very early, as a child, that a man was born with divine rights and that it was a woman's intrinsic responsibility to serve and care for him. It is unlikely he ever imagined he would find a wife who could manage their meager resources, cook like a restaurant chef, care for babies, and still work side-by-side with him in the blistering agricultural fields of California. Of course he couldn't have known this when he married his sixteen-year-old pregnant girlfriend. He married her because it was his duty, and he did always fulfill his duties, and not because he loved her, but I think she loved him madly, and she continued to do so for the next sixty years of her life.

Theirs was a traditional marriage and his role was to control her, and she complied, because that was what was expected of wives in their rural communities. Several months after they were married, they decided inexplicably, to start a journey to California, leaving on Christmas Eve, 1939. Though it was a significant and important religious day that meant a lot to Lola, she had no choice but to obey her husband. They left with very little money and no concrete plans, except to get to California to find work. They had a baby daughter and were traveling with Lola's sister Ruma, her husband Jim, and their two babies. Whenever we've asked my *Tía* Ruma why they decided to leave Canutillo for such a long trip, on Christmas Eve she would just shrug her shoulders and say, *"Pos no sé, nosotros hacíamos lo que los hombres querían."* It took them several months to arrive in Anaheim, California, and there an incident occurred that provides insight into the marital relationship of the very young Lola and the handsome Martín.

One day while the men were out working, or looking for work, Lola and Ruma were buying groceries when they came across a thrift store. They were young and loved clothes so they explored the racks of the hand-me-downs. Lola found an attractive colorful jumpsuit that she couldn't resist even though she told her sister Martín forbade her to wear pants. Possibly in defiance, she bought the outfit anyway. At the time they were living in a migrant camp, and their quarters were situated very close to one another so the young couples could easily overhear conversations. When they returned to their quarters, Lola put on her fashionable jumpsuit and was wearing it when Martín returned. She received an almost violent reaction from him. Her sister heard yelling and screaming through the tent walls and rushed in to find Lola crying with Martín threatening to remove her jumpsuit. *"Le he dicho muchas veces que no quiero que use pantalones,"* he snapped at my *Tía* Ruma. In her calm and easy manner, Ruma scolded Martín for trying to remove Lola's clothing and told Lola she shouldn't have purchased the pants knowing Martín didn't like her to wear them. He was more incensed that she had dared to disobey him, than he was with her spending their scarce financial resources. Somehow the conflict got resolved for the time being, but it was an early example of Martín's dictatorial temperament. This occurred during the first year of their marriage, during their honeymoon phase, if living in a migrant camp can be considered a honeymoon. Lola complied with Martín's wishes on that occasion, but similar scenarios were enacted throughout their marriage as Lola drifted further and further from the subordinate role expected of her.

My *Tía* Ruma narrated this story to me some sixty years after it occurred, and only she knows how the actual incident unfolded. It's possible it didn't happen exactly as she tells it. She was four years older than Lola and her memory isn't always reliable, but the story rings true to me. I visualize a scene, in black and white, of a slender young enraged man, standing over his seventeen-year-old bride, who is cowering on a dirty old army cot, ordering her to remove a piece of clothing he doesn't like. I cringe, for I remember the young woman as a sturdy boss whom no one could bend or break. Through the years many such stories about their relationship have been narrated to my sisters and me.

When their migration ended and they were settled in the San Joaquin Valley of California, they lived in the various agrarian communities of Lamont, Arvin, and Bakersfield. Their family life was tortuous, living at a bare bones level with, by now, three small children, and with Lola enduring a complete lack of confidence in Martín. There were many domestic moves; they lived in at least five different homes, shanties really, during a four year period as Martín took on a variety of agricultural and other low-paying jobs. He was adept, bright, physically strong, and developed many specialties as an agricultural laborer. During those years, he was a night irrigator, a vineyard trimmer; he picked cotton, potatoes, pruned fruit trees, and eventually became a labor leader among the Mexican workers. At times he worked as a foreman and supervised crews of workers, *braceros*, and even German prisoners of war who were temporarily held at Camp Lamont. Often the employer provided substandard living quarters for the family, but when the job was lost, Martín lost the housing as well. Frequently he experimented with his social life, behaving as a single man who had no family responsibilities. Between 1943 and 1947, Martín had several amorous liaisons that we know of which finally resulted in a marital separation that took place in the seventh year of their marriage. We've heard that he went to Los Angeles where he stayed for about six months. Lola, hardworking and resourceful, almost prospered without Martín. She established a safe stable home for herself and her daughters, found adequate employment, bought a car, and even started a savings account. Many years later, we learned that she had initiated divorce proceedings during this period, an unheard of catastrophe in the Mexican community. Lola and Martín reconciled when he returned and they appeared to have developed a strong loving relationship that held fast for many years. It is this narrative I'd like to present, the story of their love and not of their deceptions, although it is difficult to speak of one without the other.

Their lives were defined by their relationship, and when their marriage tragically ended, their lives remained forever unfulfilled. I want to believe that because of their failed matrimony, their last years were lived in lonesome regret. Theirs was not a romantic marriage but only because they didn't know how to be romantic. How does one learn romance? From the movies, popular music, or from magazines? I don't know if Martín ever sent her flowers or bought her sexy underwear, but I know he depended on her and looked upon her as his soul mate, a confidante and a comrade. Once, for her birthday or Mother's Day, he bought her a beautiful jeweled string of rosary beads, purchased in a jewelry store that also carried kitchen appliances. Lola thought it much too extravagant and immediately exchanged it for something practical, a GE mixer that she used for many years. Yet they became a team as they worked in the fields side by side and made life decisions for their family. The cliché "they were survivors" comes to mind, but they weren't survivors in the sense that they endured terrible physical suffering, which they undoubtedly did, but because they were persistent, unrelenting, they progressed, in life and in love. We may not have observed romance, but we saw jealousy so doesn't that imply romance? Even though she didn't trust him, Lola adored Martín. He was the most important man in her entire life.

I have many joyful memories of our home life and of my mother and father together from my childhood years until I left home in 1964. Visions of me happily walking to elementary school in Arvin; our *casa nueva* on Strand Street with a bedroom just for my sisters and me; my mother laughing and singing as she worked around the house; and the two of them in their own bedroom are strong emotional images that soothe me. We moved into *la casa nueva* in 1949, and it was likely the first time in their marriage that they had a bedroom of their own. Lola cared for Martín emotionally and physically; she bought every piece of clothing he ever wore, from shorts to shirts. He had only to state he was going to take a shower, and she'd quickly lay out clean clothes on the bed for him. Our new four room house was usually filled with friends and relatives, full of music from a radio console Lola received from Martín one Christmas. There was always a sense of busy social activity even though none of it was planned. When I returned home after school, I never knew if people would be visiting us and staying for dinner that evening. It's not that my parents entertained. That concept did not apply to us, our home was just always open to relatives, friends and strangers alike. After we moved to northern California, we spent a lot of time alone as a family, watching television together, going to church, and exploring the San Francisco Bay area. Even though it was a joyful time for our family, we were often lonely without our extended family around us.

After thirty-three years of marriage, that included two separations of at least six months, with one separation within the previous two years, their divorce was abrupt and painful in 1970. They were both in their forties, still young. Martín took an early retirement from the Smelting and Refinery Company that was planning to soon close down and returned to his native New Mexico. This time they gave up completely. Lola was left financially stranded and was forced to sell the house they had purchased two years earlier. She moved into a small one-bedroom apartment near the candy factory where she worked, and she quickly transformed it into a comfortable home for herself. She concealed her shame well and appeared to relish her privacy and solitude. Soon she was living what appeared to be a contented life, *sin mortificaciones* as she put it, enjoying her work, friends, and family. It was as if this was the life she'd always wanted. But she was angry, and being angry with Martín sustained her. Her fury became a source of power, similar to her prayer rituals that produced a reservoir of constancy and strength. Her victimhood became part of her character, but it didn't diminish her. In fact, like her anger it nourished her, it granted significance to her life, it provided an anchor. She would often tell us about Martín, "You don't know...*ustedes no saben todo lo que hizo.*" She hated him, but she loved him. And we had to do the same, we had to hate him but not speak badly of him. If we saw him too frequently, she'd question us and brutally tease us about the visits, especially me.

My sisters also felt a rage towards our father and didn't see him at all for eight or nine years after he moved to New Mexico. We learned that he married, then divorced then married again. I communicated with him after the birth of my daughter and reunited with him in El Paso in 1976. It was a brief visit since I was there by chance for professional reasons, but seeing him warmed my heart and I was reminded of how, regardless of his marital infidelities, he had always loved my sisters and me. I was happy to see him, and we greeted each other as loving adults. From that point on, our relationship was never quite like that of a father and daughter; he spoke to me as an equal and on various occasions revealed to me deep emotional feelings he still had for my mother. It is interesting to me now that he never exhibited any shame or remorse over his abrupt departure, leaving daughters and grandchildren behind without even a word of farewell.

I'll never understand all the reasons why he had to strive so hard at everything he did. He worked twice as hard as the average man to achieve success, success that didn't depend on brute strength, but that required planning, kindness, and working with people. Always there were details missing in his planning. A trip to California from New Mexico almost always involved an automobile mishap. While most of us have car trouble once in a while, he literally had vehicle engine trouble hundreds of times. He was often caught short of cash. He always forgot an important item, misunderstood information, and invariably had to re-do tasks. He seemed always to make mistakes, yet he never gave up. Even with all the mistakes, problems, regrets, hassles, and repercussions he experienced, it didn't stop him from trying to complete whatever he was attempting to do. Yet, like a teenager, he didn't seem to learn from his mistakes.

After our reconciliation he came to visit me one

Christmas when my marriage was failing and I was already living alone in a Berkeley duplex apartment with my young daughter. Before every trip to California he'd stock up on bottles of *tequila* that he purchased in Juarez, to bring to us as gifts. One night the two of us stayed up late talking, and drinking *tequila*. He was still a handsome man, vibrant and agile, and he confessed that he'd remarried, feeling I suppose, that an explanation was necessary. I was aware of his marriage but knew nothing of his new wife, whom I later met and accepted as his competent and devoted caretaker. As we sat in my compact kitchen in the middle of the night, downing shots of *tequila*, and as our inhibitions deserted us, he let me know how much he still loved my mother. It was unclear if he was confessing, or boasting. He would switch from Spanish to English to Spanish again and the more he drank the more he stayed with English, slurring his words, making it difficult for me to understand him. But when he spoke of love, it was in Spanish, "*yo quiero mucho a su mamá. Tambien quiero a Nena, ella es muy buena*, but I do not love her like your mother. *Nunca voy a querer a nadie como a su mamá.*" To this day I can still hear his words and see his shameless proud face. There was no embarrassment, no justification, just wide-eyed candidness.

For ten years, Martín and Lola did not communicate or see each other. Although I do remember that Lola received a letter from one of his girl friends; he continued to have many. I speculate that by visiting my sisters and me he felt close to her too, as if he were also calling on her. During those years, my daughter and I visited him in New Mexico three or four times. On one of those visits we drove into Mexico, from El Paso to Delicias, a small town south of Chihuahua, to visit one of his first cousins that he'd never met. It was a fun trip, traveling in his camper that broke down twice, and meeting distant relatives who were important to him. We stayed at the home of his cousin for

several days and toured the sights of the area. One day we
went to visit a nearby dam and made a picnic of the
occasion. After our stroll around the dam, with an ice chest
of beer and snacks, we sat under some shady trees to hide
from the hot sun. The men must have drunk more than just
beer, especially Martín and the husband of his cousin's
daughter, for we witnessed a caustic exchange between them.
The youthful husband was an odd fellow with red hair and
a freckled face that made him fairly conspicuous in the
modest western Mexican town of Delicias. Inexplicably, he
took a liking to me and managed to make a nuisance of
himself. I was divorced, in my thirties, but still pretty limited
in romantic experiences. Initially, I didn't notice that the
redhead was getting close to me, both physically and in
dialogue. After several hours of me moving away from him,
and he finding me on a bench or in a group with the other
ladies, I detected a belligerence in Martín's behavior towards
him. He just couldn't contain himself and to everyone's
embarrassment he confronted the by now sloppy drunk, and
said something like, "*tenga respeto*...keep your dirty eyes off
my daughter!" It was a mortifying moment for everyone,
especially the redhead's wife, but I felt a sense of relief since
the guy was becoming obnoxious. I appreciated my father's
protective instincts, and I looked at him gratefully, like a
little girl saved from the neighborhood bully. When the
snacks and beer vanished, our small group of seven adults
and a couple of little girls decided to eat dinner, and we
ended up in a rural unpretentious family restaurant located
nearby. We seated ourselves and had just ordered *platos
típicos regionales* from the waiter, when a three musician
conjunto appeared at our table. Politely we listened to the
unsophisticated slightly off-key guitarists and accordionist,
play and sing traditional Mexican love ballads.

The band struck up a song I'd never heard before, and
then unexpectedly, Martín leaped to his feet and placed

himself next to the musicians, joining them in singing, *"Hasta la Tumba Mujer."* He looked like a puppet, popping up suddenly to join in the singing. I don't know if he requested the song, or just joined in when he recognized it, but clearly he knew the words and gave himself totally to singing them boisterously. He was sweaty and disheveled but with his head thrown back, his eyes on me, his whole posture proclaimed the words of the love song. There was a poignant melancholiness to his behavior that pierced my heart. I couldn't remember if I'd ever heard him sing before but this behavior was unknown to me. I was sitting next to his silent wife, but it was me he looked at and I intuitively knew those love words were intended for my mother. It never occurred to me to mention the episode to her, and I didn't. Many years later I inadvertently discovered the song on a CD I picked up in Guadalajara, and was surprised at the reverent overtones of the ballad. *Hasta la tumba, mujer, juraste amarme, Hasta la tumba, mujer, tuyo he de ser. La muerte solamente ha de borrarme, El juramento de amor que hiciste ayer.* In other words, until death due us part. Martín was a romantic after all.

At the end of that summer, in 1980, my grandmother Cipriana died in Bakersfield, leaving my mother and her sisters in intense mourning. All of my grandmother's offspring were still alive except for two that had died as children. She was the mortar that held all the households together. We all gathered at her feet to adore and please her, and her death left an immense emptiness in our family's foundation. Without her presence, the family, aunts, uncles, cousins, spouses of cousins, started to scatter away from the home where she'd lived with her youngest daughter for over thirty years. My mother, grieving profoundly, spent most of her free time praying. She carried tremendous unnecessary guilt over the laborious life her mother had suffered. She felt that she and her sisters had not done enough to care for her.

At the time my sisters and I were so involved with our own families that we didn't fully comprehend the depth of Lola's pain and grief. My grandmother was eighty-two years old and had been ill for several years. She had spent the last days of her life mostly watching Mexican *novelas* on television. Nevertheless she left a powerful void in the family that would never be filled by anyone else.

Timidly, I imagine, Martín telephoned Lola when he learned of Cipriana's death. We weren't able to comfort her, but one telephone call from him, and she felt consoled and understood. Feeling shocked and sad over the death of my grandmother, he needed to express his sorrow for a woman who had treated him like her own son. In fact he always referred to her as *"Amá"* though he mysteriously called his own mother by her first name. After just one telephone call, he and Lola were not only on speaking terms, after ten years of silence, but were actually in harmony with each other as if it were 1953 all over again. My mother once stated, about her and my father, *"nos creamos juntos,"* meaning they'd grown up together. Since they were so young when they married, they'd come of age at the same time. They understood each other instantly, forgetting for the moment that Martín was married to someone else.

That Christmas, Martín came by himself to visit us. I remember my mother was very nervous about seeing him, but almost immediately she reverted to the wife role, even cooking hot *chile verde con carne* for him. They spent one night at my house, sleeping in different rooms and then went to Lola's house in Colma, south of San Francisco, for one or two nights before returning again to my home. They needed to communicate; they conversed extensively with one another. I can still recall the emotions I felt at the time; I was smugly positive they were going to be together again. One evening while they were staying with me, I went out with friends, leaving them sitting and talking at the dining room table. We had eaten dinner, and they'd stayed at the table drinking coffee and talking. I went to the movies returning about four and half-hours later, and found them still sitting in exactly the same positions, gesticulating and talking intensely. They hardly noticed me and were still there at the table when I said goodnight and went to bed.

My sisters and I accepted this scenario with untroubled complacency thinking it was meant to be. There was no doubt in our minds that they were passionately joined forever. Here they were, in love since 1938, and still behaving like youthful lovers. Lola was blooming, extra energetic, almost hyper, her happiness physically visible. Ten years of regret and loneliness had disappeared with a snap of the fingers. In fact, we all seemed to have lost ten years, shedding them like pounds, returning to the days of our youth when we were a family. But Martín had to leave, to return to New Mexico, to his job, and to his wife. During the months following his visit, they wrote regularly to each other. He sent her gifts, toiletries he could get through his job, and frequently they spoke by telephone. We could not have been more confident that they would re-marry after Martín divorced his wife; it was just a matter of time.

Inevitably, Martín invited Lola to meet him in El Paso, a city she remembered well and had always wanted to visit again. She told us of the invitation, but I, the most outspoken, replied that she'd never go since he was married and because of the significance of such a trip. They'd stay in a hotel, be alone for days, and actually it could be very romantic. She sought our approval, but we left it up to her, not making the decision easy. One Sunday morning, in September of 1981, I received a telephone call from her. Laughing happily she said, *"Donde cree que estoy?"* I said she was home, and she answered, *"...le estoy llamando de El Paso."* I didn't believe her and kept saying she was kidding and that she was only in San Francisco. Then she put my father on the phone, and he said that yes, they were both in El Paso. The wickedness of the trip plus the fact that she had deluded us delighted her and us too.

There are pictures from this trip, small Polaroid snapshots that have somehow ended up in one of my desk drawers. Martín had been using a Polaroid camera for several years and when he visited us in California he'd take pictures of his grandchildren. They loved seeing themselves instantly as the pictures gradually came into focus with their images. In El Paso, Lola and Martín were on vacation, 'paseandose sin verguenza,' eating in restaurants, going across the border to Juarez, listening to *mariachi* music, and Martín wanted to preserve these scenes. All of the pictures are of Lola. In each she is alone, since Martín was the one taking the photo. In one picture she is in a hotel room, standing in front of the window, dressed in white slacks and a rainbow striped blouse, smiling shyly. On the same day they visited a church and she is in the same clothes, standing next to the altar. It looks like St. Patrick's in Canutillo, the church where they were married in 1939. In a couple of pictures, Lola, with a drink in her hand, is standing with a group of musicians, a *mariachi* in one, and a *conjunto* in another. These are on different nights, obvious by her different outfits of low-cut or sleeveless blouses. She loved to dress sensuously, not quite sexually, but with exhilarating innocence. She possessed an innate and elegant sense of style that she radiated silently. There is a glamorous aspect to her appearance here, at the age of 59. She enjoyed wearing jumpsuits, sleeveless, or with a neck revealing bodice and her stance reflected poise and glamour.

Was she having fun? I've tried to read her facial expressions. Is she happy? She is smiling but not laughing as she often did when she was truly having fun. I have many pictures of her laughing, open-mouthed, her head back, displaying an indulgence in buffoonery, jocularity. She appreciated a good jest; wit was her forte. In these photos I find a tentativeness in her expression, a questioning of herself. Am I having fun? I wonder if she thought she was behaving immorally, having an affair with a married man. She knew Martín was being unfaithful to his wife just as he'd been unfaithful to her most of their married life.

Yet, it must have been wonderful revisiting the small towns of their early years together; Canutillo, Anthony, La Union, El Paso; having drinks in the open market in Juarez, feeling courted by a man she knew and loved. I imagine Martín was ecstatic, having her there by his side, in his world. He could boast about his new life to her and show her off too because he was proud of her. With her by his side he looked sophisticated and interesting, something his new wife couldn't do for him. Their time together was precious, nostalgic, and they had to make up for lost time. They were on the honeymoon they'd never had forty-three years earlier. After five or six days Lola flew back to her life in San Francisco.

When my mother returned from El Paso she was euphoric, according to my eldest sister, and had no regrets about visiting Martín. But her sister, my *Tía* Ruma, scolded her for being the "other woman" in the triangle, although we don't think this scolding had an impact on Lola's thinking. She was caught up in the scandalous momentum of astonishing everyone, including Martín, and couldn't care less what people thought, and she showed her daughters she could be outrageous. I can't remember that she talked to me about her trip, but she did to both of my sisters. To one of them, she mentioned that Martín wanted to set her up in an apartment in El Paso; a proposition that anyone who knew Lola understood to be preposterous. Could Martín have thought that Lola would leave her home, her daughters, and her grandchildren to be near him? I don't believe so. It was a false empty gesture on his part. To my other sister, she stated that she was just visiting him for fun, *"...y que el luego luego quería plantar rancho."* An expression unfamiliar to us, that sounded coarse coming from Lola, yet we laughed over it. Had she always just planned to have a good time, without any intention of reuniting with him? He wanted a promise of marriage from her if he were to divorce his wife, she said. Again, a ridiculous proposal since he was putting a condition upon her decision, forcing her to make a choice rather than just pursuing her passionately which is what we thought she wanted.

My sisters and I have had an infinite number of conversations over these past many years concerning our parents' love life, attempting to comprehend what happened over the next several years. What transpired right in front of our eyes that we missed? How did we misinterpret all the signals that our mother was giving us? Or maybe there weren't any signs for us to interpret because she was clear about what she wanted all along. It was we who wanted something else for her. In the end we were left bewildered and starved for knowledge. While writing these recollections, I've made a complete turnaround in my thinking about their affair. I always thought they yearned to be together, but that they just couldn't forgive one another and forget the pains of the past. Now, I don't believe my mother really wanted to return to the past. She preferred the safe and comfortable life she'd created for herself, and my father was just a disruption. I don't doubt she loved him, but she regretfully preferred a dignified and peaceful life to one of passion, turmoil and uncertainty.

Lola had a life of her own, very different from that of her sisters, and us her daughters, and almost any other woman she knew. She lived alone for almost thirty years with a few short periods of having a friend, adult grandchild, or a nephew sleeping on her sofa. A one-bedroom mobile home that didn't fit the stereotype of a trailer was her residence for most of those years. It was fashionably decorated, scrubbed as clean as a hospital, and radiated her tranquillity. She loved rearranging her furniture, hanging new drapes, and having family and friends over for dinner. In the 1970s and 1980s, she was an attractive, active, busy, socially engrossed middle-aged woman. She joined and went to a gym four evenings a week, making friends with several women members that she socialized with on the weekends. Being healthy and physically fit became almost an obsession with her. Her candy factory employment was important not just for the paycheck and union benefits but because of the friendships and social life that developed from it, plus she actually enjoyed working. During those years, she made several trips to Mexico, traveling with friends and spending weeks at the home of a longtime friend. And, she loved to dance. For many years she went dancing two or three times a weekend at the local Latino clubs and restaurants in the Mission district of San Francisco. Although shopping for clothes, for herself and her grandchildren was a pleasurable pastime, she lived modestly. Hers was a full and rich life.

Romance was not totally absent in her life either. There was an Italian man, from her workplace, who loved her. He was married and had a young son who was very important to him, but he pursued Lola. We never met him, but she spoke of him to us, although she never said if she was serious about him or not. She received him in her home where they enjoyed drinks and dinner, and conversation. We don't know if it was sexual, but it did go on for many years. I had the impression that he was waiting for his son to grow up before making a decision to leave his wife, but Lola had a casual attitude about the relationship, or she pretended to be nonchalant about it. Eventually the relationship seemed to just end, disappearing without an authentic conclusion. It had no place to go. Lola didn't appear to grieve over it.

For a few years Lola and Martín communicated with

each other regularly, by telephone and mail, but they saw each other just one more time. My paternal grandmother, Enriqueta, died in Lamont, California and my sisters, my mother and I attended the funeral services. Martín and his wife, who had always been very attentive and caring towards my grandmother, were also there. I don't know if Lola and Martín even spoke to one another on that occasion, but they did see each other. That was September of 1985, and for the next few years we saw very little of him, although one of my sisters did visit him in New Mexico during the late 1980s.

In the following years our lives became very active with new relationships and growing children, and we were negligent in paying substantial attention to Lola's world. At a very 'mature' age I shocked everyone, and myself, by becoming pregnant and having another beautiful daughter. This brought me into a committed relationship that limited the amount of time I had for my mother. My older sister's life also changed drastically when she married at the age of 49, after living as a single divorced woman for over 25 years. My mother was always with us as we entered new stages in our lives. Her life gradually slowed down when she retired from her job. It was an early retirement due to a disability she'd developed after years of moving her shoulder in a unique routine motion while hand dipping candy creams into a vat of hot rich chocolate. Initially, she was happy with her retirement, but after several years, without us really noticing it, she became dispirited and began to lose interest in the day-to-day joys of life. She moved her mobile home to the East Bay to be nearer my sister and liked the new location for a while, but slowly she found it harder and harder to keep busy. It was then that we received tragic news. Martín had a series of strokes and died in a hospital in Las Cruces, New Mexico in 1993. He was 72 years old.

As he wanted, he was buried in the poor rural cemetery

in La Union, where his grandfather rested. His five brothers, several nephews, and many cousins came together to dig his grave. Although it was a bright sunny day, a strong cold February wind blew waves of dust into the faces of the men as they took turns jumping in and out of the tomb they were preparing for him. A bottle of brandy was passed around, to warm themselves they said, but also to loosen their wit so they could joke that *El Gordo* was carefully overseeing their labor, just as he had when they'd picked grapes as young men in the fields of the San Joaquin Valley. I didn't want to look at him, as he lay in his burial bed, flawlessly made-up, mustache thinly penciled, hair neatly combed, and dressed in his best suit.

Just as his brothers had diligently dug his grave, so the whole community respectfully buried him in it. Many people we didn't know came to pay their respects. We all tossed handfuls of dirt onto the coffin. First we, his daughters, then the rest of the family, his close friends and neighbors, and finally his brothers again picked up the shovels and took turns pitching large clods of earth. The momentum picked up, as everyone wanted a turn. It became a dance and no one wanted to be left out. I didn't lift a shovel, but I've wished that I had joined in that final dance.

My sisters and I returned to California after the funeral to find our mother quiet and sorrowful. She had not expressed interest in attending the funeral and in fact spoke very little about Martín. Within a couple of years she moved into an apartment that my husband prepared for her in our home, where she lived for two years before returning to San Francisco.

essay 8

LOLA'S *ORACIONES*

Religious rituals dominated our daily lives although I don't remember feeling that we were especially spiritual. Being Catholic was like being Mexican, or being a girl; it was just who we were. Our Catholic faith was kept to ourselves, within our home life, and didn't affect our public lives. We went to Mass on Sundays because that is what one did on Sunday -- if we didn't go to Mass, it wasn't Sunday -- it had to be Saturday or some other day of the week. We didn't eat meat on Fridays; as adolescents we went to confession almost every week; we made the sign of the Cross whenever we passed a Catholic church; and we didn't eat after midnight on Saturday night if we planned to receive Communion on Sunday morning. After receiving Communion on Sunday, we'd come home and walk directly to the kitchen to get a glass of water. We'd drink exactly three swallows of water, and then we'd kiss the right hand of both of our parents. If my grandmother or an aunt was present, we'd kiss their hand too. They in turn, would give us their blessing, *"Que Dios la bendiga, mija,"* my mother might say, or maybe, *"Que Dios la cuide y que sea buena*

Rafaela G. Castro

muchachita."

My mother and grandmother's conversations were forever punctuated with many "*Ay Diosito Santo!*" "*Dios nos bendiga!*" "*Ave Maria!*" "*Si Dios da licencia,*" and "*Si Dios quiere.*" *Bendiciones* by our elders, mostly women elders, were very important and sought after by all of us as we passed through our various rites-of-passage, such as First Communion, grammar school and high school graduation, Confirmation, marriage, childbirth, and all that came afterwards. My grandmother would make the sign of the cross over our heads and recite the blessing, "*Por la señal de la Santa Cruz, de nuestros enemigos, líbranos Señor, Dios nuestro. En el nombre del Padre, del Hijo y del Espítitu Santo.*" On the day my sister got married, I remember her kneeling as my mother, my aunt, and my grandmother stood over her reciting this blessing, plus I imagine additional prayers as well. Lola's *bendiciones* became a ritual in our homes too as our children grew up and lived through their own rites-of-passage.

Dios and *Jesus, Maria y José* were our constant companions wherever we went plus we also had a huge contingent of friendly saints who were invoked, depending on the social situation or the intensity of the crisis. Just on a daily basis, we needed the La *Virgen de Guadalupe, San José, San Antonio,* and *el Santo Niño de Atocho,* or *San Martín de Porres,* or *Santiago,* and that was just to get through a single day. These were our friends who would see that our prayers reached the right deity, God, Jesus, or the Holy Ghost. I never thought of them as mystical spirits or solemn mediators that I was meant to fear. They were an extension of my family, another *Tío* or *Tía,* or maybe even a second or third cousin. If there were a serious calamity, such as an illness or a car accident, my mother and grandmother might make a vow, or a *manda,* or a *novena,* to a specific saint. Saints like St. Jude or *la Virgen de San Juan de los*

| 134

Lagos, or *la Virgen the Guadalupe* would then receive prayers on a continuous basis for nine weeks, or a sacrifice of no meat, coffee, or *pan dulce* for as many weeks. My family didn't make trips to Mexico to fulfill *mandas*, like many people we knew, though when she was much older, Lola did complete a vow to make a personal visit to a notable saint in Mexico, *La Santa Inocencia* found in the cathedral of Guadalajara.

We always had a picture of the Last Supper hanging in the kitchen of our home. In every house that we lived in, the Last Supper was perpetually there overlooking my mother's cooking, our conversations, and our kitchen activities. We never lived in a house with a dining room; otherwise the picture would have hung there, watching over us as we ate our daily *cenas*. So we always ate with Jesus and his apostles. Sometimes we had discussions about the apostles, and tried to identify them, such as Peter and Paul. My grandmother would point Judas out to us, and she identified him by the placement of his hands, held before his chest, sort of pointing to himself, as if to say, "Who me, Jesus?"

Our religious life was associated with participating in church traditions and maintaining particular cultural rituals at home, but I don't remember that we recited the rosary as a family or ever read the gospel together. Clean fresh Franciscan nuns, taught my sisters and me catechism and religious education in weekly after school classes. We memorized sections from the Baltimore Catechism handbook. Vaguely I remember some questions from the opening section. "Who made us? God made us. "Who is God?" God is the Supreme Being who made all things. "Why did God make us?" God made us to show His goodness and to share His everlasting happiness in heaven. It was reassuring simplistic indoctrination that we devoured. Nuns also provided my mother and her sister's basic religious training, but mostly they learned about Catholic traditions from their mother and grandmothers. They knew little of church history, yet their belief system was completely shaped by the religious nature of their daily lives. Personal and communal prayer was intimately incorporated into the heart of their family life. As children they were raised with a religious mind, and throughout their lives they maintained religious traditions and ritual obligations.

Lola's worldview and sense of social reality were rooted in growing up and living in poverty. Throughout her life she thought of and saw herself as a person who came from poverty, as if it were a place, a physical location that left a mark on one's psyche and body. It was a province from which one could never leave. In discussions, she'd commonly start a sentence with, "*nosotros los pobres...,*" or "*la gente pobre...*" as a prefatory qualification to a thought or position she held. The Catholic Church looked upon her community as los pobres, and it accordingly became an institution for poor people. Lola's identity was composed of *mexicanidad*, the Catholic Church, and poverty; one "holy trinity". As a young girl in Canutillo she had joined *la Sociedad Guadalupana*, a religious organization for women that provided leadership and performed works of charity. One of the first *Sociedades Guadalupana* was started in San Antonio, Texas in 1912, with a majority of the membership made up of working-class and poor Mexican American women who were devoted to *Nuestra Señora de Guadalupe*. My grandmother was very much involved in *Guadalupana* public service work in Canutillo and also in Bakersfield, California. Much of the social, religious, and cultural life of the Mexican community of Canutillo was centered on church activities. All her life my mother kept the sacred medallion given to her when she entered *la Sociedad Guadalupana*.

Our primary Christmas celebrations took place on Christmas Eve when we attended midnight mass, ate *tamales* and opened our gifts, going to bed around 3:00 or 4:00 in the morning. Christmas day was usually spent eating more *tamales* and relaxing with family. As children, we didn't expect and didn't receive many gifts, but as our family became more financially secure, our celebrations became more elaborate. On Christmas Eve, Lola worked hard to produce a huge pot of *tamales* that finished cooking as we left for *la misa de gallo* at 11:30 pm. After we became adults with our own families, my sisters and I continued to make *tamales*, as our traditional Christmas celebration, on a Saturday, inviting close friends to join us. And gradually we stopped attending *la misa de gallo* because we couldn't stay awake until 3:00 am any longer. My mother loved the busyness, excitement and urgency of holiday preparations; she loved shopping and spending leisurely days with her daughters and grandchildren after the rush of Christmas. If it had been an especially joyous holiday, she'd state, *"fue un crismes como teníamos en Canutillo."* One tradition from her childhood consisted of going house to house on Christmas day, asking the neighbors for *"¡crismes!"* The neighbors, in anticipation of the children's visits, would be prepared with candy, fruit, and baked goods that they'd place in the sacks the children carried. Lola's Canutillo childhood was always the standard for comparisons of foods, traditions, and just the general social order of the world.

Compared to Christmas, Lent and Easter were considerably more important religious holy days for Lola. She revered the discipline and physical sacrifices required of her during this sacred season. Lenten fasting was a mandate she learned from her mother that she felt compelled to follow, as if her mother were still watching over her. For 40 days she would fast and attend daily Mass. The fasting was not starvation, but meant just coffee and one piece of toast for breakfast, coffee or tea and bread for lunch, and a regular dinner, with no snacking in-between meals. Often she would also give up something she particularly liked, a food or an activity, such as dancing. When she was middle aged, she enjoyed wine with her dinner, but she abstained from all alcohol during Lent. This also meant that she wouldn't socially celebrate her April birthday, which invariably occurred during Lent. When we were teenagers she made us attend daily Mass and we unquestioningly complied. My father also acquiesced to her wishes during this time. On Friday evenings, if possible, she made us attend *El Via Crucis*, the Stations of the Cross services. As a child I spiritually absorbed the communal service of the Stations of the Cross and suffered along with Jesus his humiliations and pain. But as a teenager I remember impatiently waiting for the service to end so I could go out and meet my friends or boyfriend. Holy Week, the last week of Lent, was an especially solemn period for Lola. Usually we were on spring break from school so we had ample time to spend in church. We attended Mass every morning and the evenings too, besides Holy Thursday and the three-hour Good Friday service to listen to the Seven Last Works of Jesus Christ. Easter Sunday, the resurrection of Jesus, was a joyous occasion that we celebrated with new Easter dresses and shoes. We would have a special dinner, colored Easter eggs, and up until I married, my mother prepared an Easter basket for me.

Lola loved to reminisce about her Lenten traditions from Canutillo, where Holy Week was spent entirely in church services. She and her sisters were not allowed to do any housework, not even cooking, because it interfered with church attendance and prayer services. My grandmother prepared the household by cooking and stocking up on food early in the week, so there would be adequate time for their spiritual obligations. Structure and discipline were ingrained in my mother's approach to daily living, and this I know she acquired from her religious training and heritage. We also, my sisters and I, were beneficiaries of this heritage and learned discipline and organization from our mother. Our social lives revolved, although more loosely, around our religious legacy.

During their marriage, many friends and relatives called upon Lola and Martín to be baptismal godparents to their children. Consequently they had many *ahijadas y ahijados*, and because they were godparents they also had numerous *compadres y comadres*. Baptism, the first of the seven holy sacraments of the Catholic Church, is a momentous religious ritual and in Mexican culture calls for a serious celebration. Within two or three months of birth an infant must be baptized to cleanse his or her soul of the taint of Original Sin. If an infant should die before baptism he or she will go straight to hell, so the Church taught and my mother believed. Baptism is necessary for the salvation of the soul and for entry into heaven. In the Catholic faith the ritual consists of pouring holy water over the head of the infant with the priest stating, "I baptize you in the name of The Father, The Son and the Holy Spirit." The correct words are very important. The baptism of a first born son is frequently celebrated with the same fervor as a first marriage, with a *Mariachi* band and an abundance of food. Baptism culminates with a spiritual bonding between the child and the godparents. In turn the parents and godparents become *compadres*, life long friends who support one another through life's dilemmas and difficulties. There were many young people and adults that called my mother *madrina*, or *nina*, and *comadre*. All her life she cherished the relationships she had with her many *ahijados* and *ahijadas*.

Wherever I lived, in my various homes, my mother would frequently spend the night, and along with her clothes, she'd pack her little box of prayer books. She had a couple of these boxes that were actually old Christmas card boxes, probably from the 1960s, because they were very worn and tattered, practically falling apart. These contained not just her well read prayer books but also little slips of yellow paper, memory cards from funerals, tiny pictures of saints with prayers on the back, and everything smelled musty and holy. There may have been three or four pamphlets, stuffed with other pieces of paper and little cards, patched with tape, and a rubber band to hold them all together. She kept one such box next to her bed, wherever she slept, at her home or at mine. The prayer books and pamphlets had titles like, "The Apostleship of Prayer," *Novena consagrada a Maria Santisima de los Dolores*, "Litany of the Blessed Virgin Mary," *Novena en honor de San Martín de Porres*, "Novena in honor of Our Lady of Perpetual Help," and "Novena to St. Anthony." Her most worn prayer book was *Devocionario Católico, Practicas Piadosas con el Ordinario de la Santa Misa y Oraciones de uso diario*. It had been published in the 1940s and I've wondered if she had it since then because the pages were worn thin and the book's binding had been taped many times.

She prayed in Spanish although her prayer books were both in English and Spanish; I don't know how many prayers she knew in English besides the "Our Father" and the "Hail Mary." In her heart and soul, God was a Spanish speaker, and He understood her prayers best in the language of her soul. I don't know when she started the practice of formal daily prayer. It was possibly when I was in Brazil, because I don't remember her praying on a daily basis when I was younger. But for over thirty years, every day, she followed her own established ritual of contemplation and prayer. Sometimes it was in the morning, as she arose, or in the evening before she went to bed. Sometimes she knelt before a small shelf that held statues and pictures of her favorite saints with their own votive candles, or she might just sit up in bed and pick up her rosary beads that were always on the nightstand. She followed her own established holy litany, visibly moving her lips as she prayed. First she recited the rosary, then she prayed to all saints for their general support, then she prayed to certain saints for specific appeals; it might be *Cristo Rey,* or *la Mano Poderosa,* or *San Martín de Porres,* or *La Virgin de Guadalupe.* Her grandchildren were continually asking her for support and prayers as they took exams in school or had interviews for coveted jobs. She eagerly and lovingly agreed to intercede for them and would send prayers to the appropriate benevolent saint. When she was at my home, she'd disappear into her room, telling me, *"Voy a rezar mis oraciones."*

She often prayed *novenas,* that I tried once or twice too, but I always failed to complete the required nine days of prayer. However she was very disciplined and always completed them. I've been told the tradition of the *novena* originated with the twelve apostles and Jesus's ascension to heaven. The apostles were instructed by Jesus to pray, as they awaited the visit of the Holy Spirit. The Ascension of Jesus is celebrated in the Catholic Church on a Thursday, and Pentecost Sunday is nine days later, when the Holy Spirit appears. These nine days, or *novena,* in memory of the nine days of prayer by the apostles, have traditionally become days of prayer for a particular need or to fulfill a vow for having received a special gift. Lola frequently made *novenas* to St. Jude, for her grandchildren, or for the solving of problems in the family, such as an illness, or long-term unemployment. Her whole life she prayed for her mother, that she might rest in peace, or she prayed to her asking for assistance in dealing with us who were alive and causing Lola heartache.

Attending Sunday Mass can easily become a habit. Not necessarily a religious habit, but a custom, a comforting routine that nurtures silence and self-reflection. For me, church became a refuge, a place for contemplation and solace. I loved the murmur of Latin, looming stained glass windows, the colorful vestments, the smell of polished mahogany, the slight fragrance of stale incense, and the holy silence. Alone in church, I could release my loneliness and cry softly, or loudly if necessary. I guess I prayed sometimes, mostly to ask God for something; a boyfriend, a job, or a special favor. I was an adult before I realized that it was not my pious sensitivities that drew me into churches, instead it was the physical buildings that I treasured. I loved the physical space much more than what it represented; the house of God. Although I could be fooling myself since I don't feel the same about every church I visit. It is only the Catholic churches that transport me to a motionless wistful realm. My mother took pleasure in visiting all Catholic churches and while she lived in South San Francisco she'd often attend Mass in a different church each Sunday. She performed a faith ritual in churches, that she passed on to us. She told us that every time we visited a Catholic church for the first time we were to recite three "Our Fathers," and make three wishes. Throughout our travels, in the U.S., Mexico and Europe, my eldest sister and I continue to perform this ritual.

After high school, I attended an over-priced six-month dental assistant training course in San Francisco. Soon, after many prayers and lit votive candles, I secured employment with a cranky old male dentist in Oakland. His practice consisted of three rooms; his office, the waiting room and the room with the dreaded dental chair. Consequently, we worked in very close proximity. Many of his patients were African American children referred by the county welfare department. He was my first encounter with a mean spirited verbally abusive old man. To get to my job, I rode a Greyhound bus for an hour, ending my journey at the bus station in downtown Oakland. Across the street from the station, on San Pablo Avenue, was St. Francis de Sale Cathedral that I visited every day as I walked the four blocks to my job. It was usually dark, after the last morning Mass, but it felt familiar to me and still smelled of burning candles. I'd sit and cry silently, praying, maybe even wishing for the death of the evil old dentist. The utter stillness of the cathedral was the perfect place to cry and pray; those visits consoled me and gave me courage to act. Six weeks was all I could take; then I swiftly decided I'd rather work as a dental technician, away from ill-tempered dentists. My prayers were answered when I found employment with a large private dental laboratory just one block away from the old dentists' office where I worked for two years. From my mother, I inherited faith in the power of prayer.

Lola exhibited a contradictory skepticism towards life, which she may have inherited from her mother. While she held a strong belief in the ability of prayer to spiritually enhance life, a life believed to be doomed from birth to toil and hardship, she also adhered to an unwavering negativism about human behavior, especially male human behavior. Somehow her reliance on prayer to guide and enhance her life managed to be the stronger of these antithetical sentiments.

It just happened that a few weeks before the death of my father, my husband and I had moved into a large older home that we had loved at first sight. We had particularly liked it because of a downstairs in-law apartment that my husband eventually expanded and meticulously remodeled especially for my mother. He installed a new floor, new kitchen cabinets, new carpeting and fresh white paint. For years there'd been an unspoken agreement among my sisters and I that ultimately my mother would live with me. At last, we were happy when she was able to move into her own place within my home, near her youngest granddaughter and near me. I felt as if I had at last completed my quintessential commitment to my mother. We'd come full circle, reaching the point where we'd been when I left for Brazil thirty-one years earlier. Once she was settled in, I'd stop by her apartment every day to say good morning, as I left the house for work. She'd be praying, or eating breakfast, and it would warm my heart that she was safe and comfortable under the protection of my home. It seemed so right, I thought. Our worlds were moving in the correct trajectory, towards a time of peace and tranquility as she entered her elderly years.

There had been a time when we'd been especially close, after I was divorced, had my own home and lived alone with my young daughter. In those years she'd had a key to my house and could come anytime without asking, and she did. She hadn't approved of my failed marriage, a Catholic marriage, but she had liked that I was easily accessible to her, with no man around to absorb my attention. Even though she didn't hesitate to criticize my way of life sometimes, I remember those years as a cherished time in our relationship. She knew many of my friends, enjoyed them, and they in turn had liked her. We had socialized together and been like equal adults. But the years passed and after many changes in my life, another husband and another child, I was now looking forward to a similar sense of closeness. This time though we were happy together for only a short time. Before my very eyes she dramatically and inexplicably became a different person.

After just a few months, she started complaining about the house, that it was too big, and it's location too isolated. It was too cold, too windy, too far from a commercial area, and the neighbors were not friendly. Although she had no serious illnesses her customary ailments loomed larger and more dramatic than before and she was constantly keeping doctor's appointments. Initially she'd join us for breakfast or dinner, until she decided she didn't like our cooking, or we ate dinner too late for her, and gradually she came upstairs less and less. My oldest daughter was now away at college, and my young daughter was seven or eight years old. Every evening after putting her to bed I'd go downstairs and watch television for an hour or so with my mother. I desperately wanted her to be happy. If she couldn't be happy then I wanted her to at least be comfortable and content with her life. But I couldn't will her happiness, couldn't do anything to change how she felt. She was falling into a depression and I wasn't aware of it, and neither were my sisters. All we saw was behavior that seemed to become more and more irrational.

She would tell our friends, and her own sisters, that she didn't like living in her apartment, didn't like living in our house. In a short time, within the year, she thought of moving to Bakersfield, near her sisters, an idea that had not occurred to her in the forty-three years since we'd moved away from there. She took a trip to Mexico to visit the small *pueblo* of one of her best friends, a place she'd visited before and loved, and where she was treated like a famous pop idol. She returned one week early because she wasn't having a good time, she was bored. We proposed a party to celebrate her seventy-fifth birthday but she refused. When she had turned seventy she'd also refused a party, telling us to wait until she turned seventy-five. Now she told us she didn't want a party, *"por que la gente me va mirar,"* and *"no quiero que me miren."* We couldn't understand her sentiments and she wasn't able to explain exactly how she felt, but it was clear we couldn't do anything to change her mind. Instead of a party the whole family, including grandchildren and their spouses, took her to dinner to a nice restaurant in the Oakland marina.

In our family, death was a topic openly discussed and humorously accepted. It was inevitable and not feared personally, yet we all greatly mourned the loss of close relatives; our father, favorite cousins, and our grandmothers.

For years my mother had frequently spoken of her own death. Sometime during this period she asked my sister to write down how she wanted her funeral arranged. It could have been macabre, but she gained comfort from having all the details known in advance. Many years before she'd purchased a burial plot in a Bakersfield cemetery, when she decided she wanted to be buried near her mother, Cipriana. With so much family in Bakersfield and the surrounding areas, we knew it was the right place for her. But suddenly, references to her own death multiplied and took on a premonitory tone. Her statements resonated with an emphatic certainty, as if she were planning a trip and had already made travel arrangements. A conversation with one of us or one of her grandchildren followed a similar pattern:

"I'll see you next week grandma," a granddaughter might say.

"I'll don't know if I'll be here," she'd respond.

"Why, where are you going?"

"I might be dead," she'd say, or else, "I'm going to die."

We got used to it and would laugh nervously but we didn't recognize the increase in her obsession with death until some years later.

Unexpectedly, she notified me that she'd bought a small trailer she found advertised somewhere and was having it moved to a trailer park in South San Francisco. I found it hard to believe her. It just didn't make sense to me. Her plan was to return to where she had once lived, before she'd retired, near her old friends, although many of her old friends had moved or died. Unwavering, she went ahead and sold all of her furniture, living room and bedroom sets, because she wouldn't need them in the trailer that had built-in furniture. Once her mind was made up she was in a hurry to leave, as if she were fleeing a dangerous situation. I felt betrayed, at a loss, trying to understand why she didn't want to live with my family, with me. I could only see that she was leaving my home and my love; she was rejecting me. I wondered why God did not intercede.

Once she was settled, I couldn't bear to see her living in the small dreadful trailer, and I only visited there twice. Her living situation pained me and inflamed my disappointment and anger. How she could have given up a nice apartment for a camping trailer I couldn't understand. Her behavior appeared normal, and she seemed happy, flinging herself into forming a new life in a new location. I remembered how she always liked fresh starts, new beginnings. Yet her living conditions belied normality, her home was regressive, transitory and depressing. It was a claustrophobic box, unattractive and frightful. She lived there six months before she died.

It was an accident. The small trailer stove used propane gas and she forgot to turn it off while she recited her prayers. Gradually she fell asleep. It happened on a Friday night and we, my sisters and I, called her all weekend until finally extremely worried we called the police to check on her on Sunday afternoon. A tall votive candle was still burning. We never saw her.

It was sudden and unforeseen. My sisters and I were in shock, as were her two surviving sisters. One was four years older than she was, the other four years younger. They were not prepared to say goodbye. Her body was taken to Bakersfield and she was laid to rest at the feet of her beloved mother. A *Mariachi* band played during the Mass that was held at the St. Clemente Mission, and one of her nieces beautifully sang "Amazing Grace." Everything was just as Lola requested.

I suffered immense anguish, and also indignation. I felt rejected, left behind. She had left me twice. First when she had moved out of my home, seeped in unhappiness, and then when her life abruptly ended. Consciously and deliberately she had removed herself from my life. Her best friend Maria came from Mexico for the services and she spent one night with me. She consoled me by saying Lola had died exactly as she'd prayed for; in her sleep, and that she had been well prepared, faithfully and devoutly, to meet her God. She had prayed for death and God had listened to her.

essay 9

DESPEDIDA

I will always think of myself as an Arvin girl; as a working class daughter. During my life I have often felt like an apprehensive wallflower hesitant to make waves; fearful of drawing attention to herself and possibly inciting anger in someone, anyone. Much of my life has been lived as a secluded bystander, an observer of historical and social events; the 1960s, Berkeley, the Vietnam War, the Civil Rights movement. There has never been a defining moment in my life engendered by the music of the Beatles, or the lyrics of a Bob Dylan song. I have been that silent person on the sidewalk, observing the boisterous protesters marching down the street. Although the Peace Corps changed the course of my life, I've often felt like an exile, a sojourner, a non-native, yet not quite an immigrant. There were times when I felt that I participated fully in the present moment, such as the Peace Corps and when I volunteered with the United Farm Workers Union. My father felt great pride that I met and worked for Cesar Chavez, albeit for a brief period. But mostly I have wanted to be unnoticed, left alone to follow my own script, to seek my own contradictory fantasies and indulgences. My life, now into the last quarter stretch, has felt paralyzed, on-hold as I've fulfilled the responsibilities anticipated of me. I've executed the obligations expected of me by my religion, by my culture, by the society that socialized me, and by my mother.

It might be presumptuous of me to attempt to engagingly narrate the story of a socially marginal family, the love story of a Latino man and woman. Not because the story is not authentic and universal but because of the difficulty in conveying such a story in the language of love and intimacy. My rhetorical capacity to compose the story of my mother and father is limited. My first language became crippled early in my childhood, and my adopted written language has yet to reach the esteemed position that invites respect.

I've written these essays as exercises, as part of a journey, a pilgrimage, with the destination being to comprehend the life that was created for me and that I've begrudgingly, but obligingly pursued. Reciting memories and composing word narratives has provided me a passage to grieving and to a final acceptance of the end of two vital lives. To most of society Lola and Martín may have been invisible but to my worldview they were formidable giants. In these writings I've striven to translate their lives, uncover the resolutions to their problems, decipher answers to the mysteries of their decisions, all to reach an understanding of their love for one another and the impact that love had on their daughters. These are the recurrent stories I repeated to myself, as I became more and more engrossed in their lives, and in the legacy they left behind: their daughters, and their daughters' children. Of the three daughters, two of us inherited the inability to make sound judgments in selecting husbands and divorced early in our first marriages. Our second choices were sound and appear to be long lasting. In our careers, all three of us completed professional degrees and practiced service careers in education and law.

Leaving home, when I did at the age of twenty, resulted in the formation of a silent, melancholic covenant between my mother and me, which defined our relationship for the rest of our lives. It never would have occurred to me to imagine I had a special relationship with her if I hadn't spent those years far away from her. My absence granted her the occasion to mourn for me. I didn't move out of our home to live nearby, I moved halfway around the world and because of that distance, I became a reluctant martyr. She wrote me intimate sensitive letters brimming with ardent words she could never have expressed verbally to me, and possibly, not even to herself. Her expressions of love, feelings of loss, blessings for me, could only be proclaimed because I was thousands of miles away. She didn't come from a family that openly professed loving feelings to one another so she couldn't have taught us to be expressive about our own emotions. Yet somehow I learned to tell her that I loved her. Our two year separation set us on a course we could not have created ourselves and determined our relationship into my middle age and up to her death. I still think she believed she possessed a fundamental authority over my life, because I was the youngest child or because she'd shared intimate introspections with me. But through the long years, each turn in the road led us more deeply into a relationship of unfulfilled expectations.

For me, the question arises, how is it that I garnered the inclination and the courage as a young woman, to leave my home and my mother? Friends and family members alike have told me it was preordained; it was meant to be. It was fate. My desire for a *provocación* did not originate in my teenage mind, but in my childhood mind, perhaps in Arvin, as I meandered crying through the foggy school playground experiencing my first existential crisis. Yet, if this is the case, why did I not continue searching for *provocaciones* throughout my life? Or did I? Why do I feel that I've acquiesced to a future contrived by others?

Years later, as an adult, when I became fully aware of my mother's frailties and weaknesses, I felt a frustrated anger towards her. I only wanted to see her strong and sure of herself. When she wrote me of her feelings about my father, I was appalled and felt embarrassment. I resented that she thought it correct to share her feelings about my father with me, her young inexperienced daughter. I felt inappropriately drawn into their tumultuous relationship, and it opened the door for me to declare my disappointments with both of them. Many of the letters I wrote from Brazil overflowed with advice about their relationship. Was this the *provocación* I had been searching for? It was painful to see my mother as less than the undaunted image I had created of her all my life.

Only after many discussions about our mother's life and death did my sisters and I realize that she had been depressed and disheartened the last few years of her life. Something triggered her depression, and I've convinced myself that it was the death of my father. It was during the year after his death, I later realized, that her behavior became peculiar with a rapidly accelerating depression that she couldn't shake off. At the time of his death, they hadn't seen each other for several years although they may have still spoken by telephone periodically. But he was still in this world, and possibly she drew comfort from that knowledge. Even though there was no thought or inclination of reuniting with him, his existence, his being, provided her life with sustenance. After his death, she must have felt a terrible loneliness knowing he was gone forever, knowing there was now no place to secure the love/hate emotions she still suffered for him. I imagine losing Martín might have felt like losing a person who has been terminally ill or in a coma for many years. That person may have been lost years earlier, but his body was still alive, and that body furnished consolation. Death came prematurely to Martín and robbed Lola of that consolation. For years there had been no relationship with him, but their history together was so fervently powerful that it dominated her life, and survived in her heart throughout the years of separation. With him physically gone, she may have thought she had no reason to live, and an unbearable depression paralyzed her ability to make a new life, a life without the essence of Martín. It is difficult not to believe she died of a broken heart, four and a half years after his death.

I cannot think of a more mysterious and complicated relationship than that between a mother and her child. The relationship must change and evolve as the mother and the child grow up, grow apart, but the immutable bond can never dissolve. It is the substance of novels, psychotherapy, murder, television sitcoms, and passionate extended conversations among adults. My mother dominated my life just by existing – by being my mother. She was the most fascinating woman I've ever known, and a day doesn't go by that she doesn't enter my life in some way, in my thoughts or my dreams. I wanted her to let me love her and take care of her, wanted her to love me and take care of me. I wanted us to have a mutual respect for each other, but it couldn't happen. That would have made our lives easier. She was an enigmatic person, independent and strong, opinionated and critical. I felt she wanted to put me in a box and care for me, but I was too independent and opinionated and critical. Starting as a child, whenever I was away from her I was afraid I'd commit a sin, do something terribly wrong. I'd get a nauseous feeling in the pit of my stomach if I thought I committed a wrong that would result in her disapproval. So as not to do wrong, I divulged everything to her -- or so I thought. Once, when I had a steady lover, I feared she'd know what I was doing. Actually, I pretended that she didn't know because I thought she believed I could do no wrong, but the pain in my stomach was constant and persistent.

For several years I was furious with her for leaving me, angry because I knew she wanted to die. It was so selfish of her. But now I realize that to her, the purposes of her life had been fulfilled and she was ready to leave. My anger has subsided and is not as potent anymore. These days I just miss her. I've accepted the truth that the person in this world who most cared for me in life is no longer present on this earth. She left me an orphan, left me alone at sea struggling and treading water with no anchor to tether myself to, with no bond to the world of my childhood.

glossary

MEXICAN WORDS AND PHRASES

ahijadas y ahijados – goddaughters and godsons
allí está la casa de Di Giorgio – there is Di Giorgio's house
un americano – an American
americanos ricos – rich Americans
Los Amoles – soap weed; a bulb used to make soap
un andariego – wanderer; traveler
arracadas – hoop earring
¡Ave Maria! – Hail Mary
avena – oatmeal
Ay hija no quiero mortificarla con mis penas, pero con platicarle descanso un poco – Oh, daughter, I don't want to trouble you with my problems, but by conversing about them, I can rest a bit
¡Ay Diosito Santo! – Oh, my blessed little God
¡Ay, que fea! – Oh, how ugly
¡Ay, que greñuda está! – Oh, your hair is very messed up
¡Ay, que tonta! – Oh, how dumb of you
Ay, se me salió el gas – Oh, gas escaped from my body; gas left me

Ay viene la muchacha más bonita de Arvin – here comes the
   prettiest girl in Arvin

bençáo – blessing (Portuguese)

bendición – blessing

braceros – Mexican guest workers, laborers, from 1942 to
   1964

¿Bueno Martín, cuando nos vamos? – Well Martin, when do
   we leave?

calzones – underpants

Cantinflas – theatrical name for Mexican comedic actor
   Mario Moreno

la casa de lamina – the house of aluminum

la casa nueva – the new casa

cascarón – eggshells decorated in bright colors and filled
   with confetti

cenas – dinners

El Chamizal – A strip of land, along the Rio Grande on the
   border between El Paso, Texas and Juarez. The Rio
   Grande River shifted courses over the years and 600
   acres that originally belonged to Mexico became U.S.
   territory. When President John Kennedy visited Mexico
   in1963 he agreed to give this territory back to Mexico.

chile – chile peppers

chile verde con carne – green chiles with meat

chones – underpants

comal – heavy flat griddle for cooking tortillas

como le gusta averiguar a ésta muchacha – how this girl likes
   to argue

compadres y comadres – co-fathers and co-mothers; spiritual
   relationship between the child's parents and the god
   parents

cosas de mujer – things pertaining to women

conjunto mexicano – group of three or four musicians
   playing northern Mexico music; Texas-Mexican music

cuando me dejó y se fue para Brasil – when you left me and
    went to Brazil

Dales puro frijoles – give them only beans

Despedida – farewell; leave-taking

*Devocionario Católico, Practicas Piadosas con el Ordinario
    de la Santa Misa y Oraciones de uso diario* – Devotional
    Catholic Prayer book, Pious Practices with the Standard
    of the Holy Mass and Prayers for daily use

disgustada – displeased; unhappy

dicho – folk saying; proverb

Dios nos bendiga! – God bless us

doença de infância – infant's illnesses (Portuguese)

¿Donde cree que estoy? – where do you think I am

emfermedades de mujer – women's illnesses

en un rancho – on a ranch, in the country

era muy traviesa – she was very mischievous; naughty

esa blusa esta muy arrugada, quítesela – that blouse is very
    wrinkled, take it off

estan malas – they are ill; they are ailing

extranjero – stranger; foreigner

familia – family

festa – party (Portuguese)

fue un crismes como teníamos en Canutillo – it was a
    Christmas like we used to have in Canutillo (Texas)

gallo – rooster; cock

la gente pobre – the poor people

el Gordo – the chubby one

una gran provocación – a great provocation

la Güera - the light skinned one

hablar con la f – speak with the letter F

un hacendado – a landowner; a rancher

Rafaela G. Castro

Hasta la Tumba Mujer – Until the tomb, woman/wife
  Hasta la tumba, mujer, juraste amarme,
  Hasta la tumba, mujer, tuyo he de ser,
  La muerte solamente ha de borrarme,
  El juramento de amor que hiciste ayer.
  Until the tomb, woman, you swore to love me
  Until the tomb, woman, I will be yours
  Only death can remove the
  The oath of love you made yesterday
el idioma de la f – the language of the F
jaitón – derives from 'high-class'; a snob
jamaica – Catholic fund raising bazaar
kimona – bathrobe
le estoy llamando de El Paso – I am calling you from El Paso
Le he dicho muchas veces que no quiero que use pantalones
  – I've told her many times that I don't want her to wear
  pants
la loca – the madwoman; the crazy one
Lola Beltran – Mexican singer and film actor of the 1940s
  and 1950s
Lola está muy nerviosia – Lola is very nervous
La Loma barrio – Mexican neighborhood of Bakersfield
madrina – godmother
manda – an offering; a vow
mariachi – musical group that plays the most traditional
  music associated with Mexico
El matrimonio es la cruz de la mujer – marriage is the cross
  woman must bear
mayordomo – overseer; supervisor of agricultural workers
me estoy volviendo loca aquí – I am going crazy here
mexicanidad – a sense of self-identity with a Mexican
  consciousness
Mi cuerpo no me pide agua – my body doesn't ask for water
La migra – the U.S. Border Patrol

Mija, no se vaya, no deje a su mamá – my daughter, don't go, don't leave your mother

la misa de gallo – midnight mass

muchachito – little boy

una mujer mala – a bad woman; a prostitute

muy habladora – very talkative

muy volada – infatuated with oneself; very passionate over a girl/boy

no quiero que me miren – I don't want them to look at me

No tengo ganas de cocinar – I don't feel like cooking

nomas le pido a Dios que cuando vuelva a Rodeo no eche menos la casa. Nomas acuerdese que en esa casa me quise morir de tresteza por su ausencia, ni me quiero ni acordar. – I only pray to God that when you return to Rodeo you won't miss the house. Just remember that in that house I wanted to die of sadness from missing you, I don't even want to remember it.

nos creamos juntos – we were raised together

Nosotros los mejicanos esto – *nosotros los mejicanos aquello* – we the Mexicans this, we the Mexicans that

nosotros los pobres – we the poor

novelas – soap operas

novena – ninth

Novena consagrada a Maria Santisima de los Dolores – Sacred Novena to the Most Holy Mary of Sorrows

Novena en honor de San Martín de Porres – Novena in honor of St. Martin of Porres

Nuestra Señora de Guadalupe – Our Lady of Guadalupe

Nunca voy a querer a nadie como a su mamá. – I will never love anyone like I love your mother.

Oraciones – prayers

pan de levadura – yeast bread

pan dulce – sweet bread; Mexican bread

Pancho Villa's Dorados – Elite troops and bodyguards of Pancho Villa, known as 'The Golden Ones'

Rafaela G. Castro

pedo – fart

Pedro Armendarez – Mexican film actor of the 1940s, 1950s, and 1960s

Pedro Infante – Mexican singer and film actor of the 1940s. He died in 1953 in a plane crash and was mourned by all of Mexico.

paseandose sin verguenza – traveling, enjoying themselves without shame

pienselo bien – think it well; think it through

platicar – to converse

platicadora – conversationalist

platos típicos regionales – typical regional plates

Por la señal de la Santa Cruz,
de nuestros enemigos, líbranos Señor, Dios nuestro.
En el nombre del Padre, del Hijo y del Espítitu Santo.
By the sign of the Holy Cross
Save us from our enemies, Lord, Our God
In the name of the Father, the Son, and the Holy Spirit

por que la gente me va mirar – because people will look at me

Pos no se, nosotros hacíamos lo que los hombres querían. – Well, I don't know, we did what the men wanted

pueblo – town

que le hiso un daño – that he harmed her; that he caused her damage

Que Dios la bendiga, mija. – May God bless you, my daughter.

Que Dios la cuide y que sea buena muchachita. – May God take care of you and may you be a good little girl.

¿Que pasó mija, la tumbó el gallo? – What happened daughter, did the rooster knock you down?

¿Quién es la muchacha más bonita de Arvin? – Who is the prettiest girl in Arvin ?

a ranchera – a style of song reflecting rural sentiments; a country ballad *los rancheros nos trataban bien* – the growers treated us well

retrato – picture; photograph

se alivió – she is healed; she has recovered

se la robó – he stole her; he kidnapped her

se me cansa la lengua – my tongue gets tired

se va enfermar por cinco días – you will be ill for five days

se va lastimar – you are going to hurt yourself

señorita – a young woman; an unmarried woman; a virgin

señoritas viejas – spinsters; little old ladies

sertão – backland; desolate interior of northeast Brazil (Portuguese)

Si Dios da licencia – If God gives us license

Si Dios quiere – If God wants

si, fue el gallo – yes, it was the rooster (that knocked me down)

sitios – rural communities (Portuguese)

sin mortificaciones – without humiliating problems

la Sociedad Guadalupana – Society of Guadalupe

Su mamá que la Quiere Mucho y no la Olvida – Your mother that loves you very much and never forgets you

También quiero a Nena, ella es muy buena – I also love Nena, she is a very good person

tacos – corn or flour tortillas folded after filled and with meat, chile, cheese

tamales – corn dough, stuffed with pork or chicken, cooked in a corn husk

telenovela – Mexican TV soap opera

tenga respeto – show respect; have respect

tenía granos en la cabeza – you had pustules on your/the head

tequila – Mexican liquor distilled from fermented juices of the agave plant

tía, tío – aunt; uncle

tina – a metal tub used for washing clothes, or for holding iced drinks and watermelons *traviesa* – troublesome; mischievous; naughty kid

Los Tres Diamantes – a Mexican trio singing group formed around 1948

tortillas – round, thin, pancake shaped bread made from wheat or corn flour

tú – intimate form of you

usted – polite form of you

usted se creé muy buena como que no nececita mi ayuda – you think of yourself as perfect, as if you don't need my help

Usted tiene la sangre muy débil – your blood is very weak

ustedes no saben todo lo que hizo – you don't know everything that he did

El Via Crucis – the Stations of the Cross

Voy a rezar mis oraciones – I am going to recite my prayers

y apoco se creé muy bonita – and I suppose you think of yourself as very pretty

y que el luego luego quería plantar rancho – and he right away wanted to create a ranch; shack up

Yo quiero mucho a su mamá – I love your mother very much